REFERENCE

LANDS and
PEOPLES

SPECIAL EDITION:
CRISIS IN THE MIDDLE EAST

GROLIER

LANDS and PEOPLES

SPECIAL EDITION:
CRISIS IN THE MIDDLE EAST

STAFF

Lawrence T. Lorimer . . . . .Editorial Director
Joseph M. Castagno . . . . .Executive Editor
Richard W. Bulliet . . . . .Text Author
Doris E. Lechner. . . . . .Director, Annuals
Lisa Holland. . . . . .Editor
Karen A. Fairchild . . . . .Editorial Assistant
Stephan Romanoff. . . . . .Proofreader
Jeffrey H. Hacker . . . . .Managing Editor
Tone Imset Ruccio. . . . . .Art Director
Elizabeth Farrington . . . . .Art Assistant
Jeanne A. Schipper. . . . . .Production Editor
Ann Eriksen. . . . . .Chief, Photo Research
Elissa G. Spiro. . . . . .Photo Researcher
Pauline M. Sholtys . . . . .Chief Indexer
Joseph J. Corlett. . . . . . . .Director of Manufacturing
Christine L. Matta . . . . .Senior Production Manager
Pamela J. Murphy . . . .Assistant Production Manager
A. Rhianon Michaud . . . . . . .Production Assistant

ISBN 0-7172-8015-2

Printed in the United States of America

MAY 0 4 1993

Contents

The U. S. and its allies emerged victorious from the Persian Gulf War. Now the world waits in hope to see what good might eventually arise from the conflict's terrible death and destruction.

CRISIS IN THE MIDDLE EAST:
The Underlying Issues

On February 27, 1991, President George Bush ordered a halt of offensive military actions: Operation Desert Storm had ended. The victorious U.S.-led Allied coalition had liberated Kuwait, and a new era in the history of the Middle East was at hand. Ever since Iraq invaded Kuwait on August 2, 1990, Middle East specialists had made predictions about what might happen if war came to the Persian Gulf region. Now their predictions were due for testing.

It will be months, perhaps years, before the full impact of the Persian Gulf War can be assessed. The objective of this book is not to repeat old predictions, but to explain why the war will likely become a turning point in the region's history. The heightened importance and involvement of the United States as a participant in Middle East politics is a key element in the new situation. Equally important is the unexpected merging of a number of complex regional and international factors.

After presenting an overview of the Middle East as a region, we will outline the development of the most crucial factors in the maze of Middle East crises—Nationalism, Zionism, Islam, Terrorism, Oil, and The Cold War—and then describe the way in which they all converged during and after the Persian Gulf War.

The Middle East as a Region

Although the word "middle" in the term Middle East is often explained by showing that the region forms the crossroads between Europe, Africa, and Asia, the phrase actually gained popularity only during World War II. Prior to that time, the common term in English was Near East. After all, the Near East was the nearest part of the East, or Orient, the term by which Europeans and Americans designated all of the cultures and peoples of Asia, a continent whose religions, languages, and customs seemed, from the Euro-American perspective, alien, backward, and more than a little scary. The Near East, however, traditionally included all of the Ottoman Empire, a multi-ethnic Islamic state that in 1800 ruled not only the countries that today make up Turkey and most of the Arab states, but also Greece and many of the Balkan nations to its north.

In the course of the 19th century, all of the largely Christian Balkan countries won independence from the Ottoman Sultan, sometimes after hard-fought wars, and were accepted as part of Europe. Then, during World War II, the new nations succumbed to invading forces from Germany and Italy. By agreement with the United States, the British assumed primary military responsibility for liberating the Axis-occupied lands in the eastern Mediterranean region and, to that end, established a major logistics center in Egypt. The British called it the Middle East Supply Center.

With the end of the war, most of the Balkan states fell under Soviet domination and thus continued their separation from the lands of the Turks, Arabs, and Persians. So the name Middle East stuck and, for convenience, was also applied to the countries of North Africa which share a linguistic and ethnic identity with the Arab parts of the Middle East, and adhere to the religion of Islam. Thus the Middle East, by many current definitions, stretches as far west as Morocco, a country whose territory reaches farther west than any part of Europe or the British Isles.

Though administrative convenience more than geography gave rise to the term Middle East, the region nonetheless deserves to be considered as a whole. Its dominant religion is Islam, even though there are significant Christian minorities in countries like Egypt, Lebanon, and Syria, and Israel is predominantly a Jewish state. Linguistically, Arabic is spoken in all but three countries—Turkey, Iran, and Israel. Persian (or Farsi), the language of Iran, is entirely unrelated to Arabic grammatically, but it uses the same alphabet and contains many words borrowed from Arabic. Likewise, Turkish contains many Arabic and Persian loanwords even though its grammar differs completely from either of those languages. Up to the 1920s, Turkish was written in Arabic script, although now it uses the same letters we do. As for Hebrew, even though its writing system is different, its grammar and many of its words are similar to Arabic.

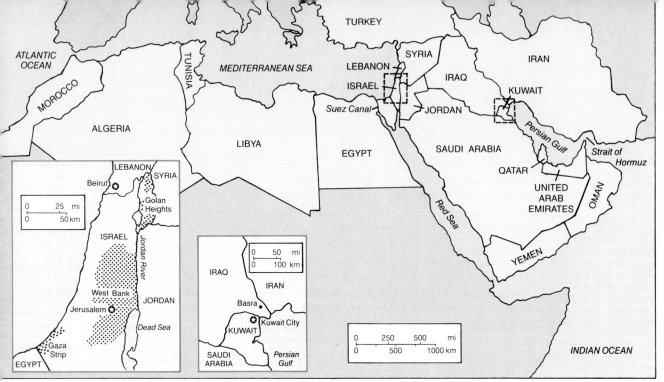

The term "Middle East" is used by Americans and other westerners to describe most of North Africa and southwest Asia—a region whose residents share similar religious and cultural traditions.

History, too, binds the Middle East into a coherent region. In the 7th century A.D. the Prophet Muhammad founded the Islamic religion on the basis of revelations he and his followers considered divine. In the decades after his death in A.D. 632, Islam spread from Spain to India, first as a conquering empire ruled by Arabs and then, gradually, through the voluntary conversion of the conquered peoples. Thus for 14 centuries, Islam has been at the core of a religious, political, and cultural experience shared by Arabs, Turks, and Persians alike. In Israel, too, the majority of the Jewish population is descended from Jews who grew up in countries formed by the history and culture of Islam, even though Zionism, the political movement that founded the country, originated in Europe and was guided to success by European Jews.

The last great empire in the Middle East was that of the Ottomans, a Turkish princely family that in A.D.1300 governed only a small part of what is today northwestern Turkey. Within 300 years, however, Ottoman armies had fought their way to the tip of Arabia in the south, the border of Iran in the east, the Moroccan frontier in the west, and the gates of Vienna in the north. Of today's Middle East, only Iran, Morocco, and some parts of the desolate Arabian peninsula retained independence from Ottoman rule.

When the Ottoman government decided to enter World War I on what proved to be the losing side, no one dreamed that within a decade the empire would be divided into many separate countries. Ottoman weakness was nevertheless apparent in the empire's progressive loss, not only of its Greek and Balkan provinces to independence movements, but also of its vast North African possessions to French and Italian imperialism.

Nationalism

The rise of nationalism, the dominant political force in the Middle East during the first two-thirds of the 20th century, owed much to Europe. On the one hand, British, French, and Russian imperialism posed an ever-growing threat that inspired certain Middle Eastern leaders with a passion to preserve or free their lands from European control. On the other hand, Italian and German nationalist thinkers and leaders had finally united their divided countries into strong states during the latter part of the 19th century. Such nationalist success stories provided examples of how to instill feelings of political solidarity in people of similar language and culture and use those feelings to attain political goals.

The roots of the various Middle Eastern nationalisms, most notably those of the Turks and the Arabs, lay in the 19th century with those thinkers who stressed the importance of native language, rather than religion, as the primary source of people's political identity. World War I gave these nationalist feelings room to grow. With the Ottoman empire defeated, eager nationalist leaders voiced demands for independence based on language and ethnic tradition. Some, like the Armenians and the Kurds, met with little success. But the dynamic leadership of Mustafa Kemal Atatürk did bring a new nationalist Turkish republic into existence in the old Ottoman heartland.

Arab nationalism was initially frustrated by the imposition or continuation of British and French control over most of the Arab world. Circumstances differed from Algeria, which was heavily colonized and legally annexed to France, to Egypt and Iraq, where the British dominated semi-independent monarchs. But everywhere, nationalist hatred of imperialism burned in the breasts of the Arabs.

Exhausted by World War II, France and Britain reluctantly gave up their imperialist ambitions. Some countries they left more-or-less voluntarily—in this way Lebanon and Syria became independent of France—

The British and French dominated much of the Middle East before World War II. The U.S. is often viewed by Middle East peoples as the imperialistic successor to the old colonial powers.

while other countries had to fight for their freedom. The fiercest fight was in Algeria, where the nationalist movement expelled the French after a vicious war. In Egypt, nationalist forces led by Gamal Abd al-Nasir (Nasser) overthrew the monarchy in 1952. Then, in 1956, Nasser had to fight off a coordinated Israeli/British/French invasion that sought to overthrow him under the guise of repossessing the formerly European-owned Suez Canal (which Nasser had nationalized).

In 1971, the formation in the lower Persian Gulf of the United Arab Emirates from a group of seven small states previously under British control marked the final achievement of Arab independence. But one of the greatest goals of the early nationalist thinkers had still not come to pass: the union of all the Arabs into one great Arab nation. Attempts at union, such as that between Syria and Egypt between 1958 and 1961, had failed. With the passage of time, the Arabs came increasingly to accept the likelihood that the borders between them drawn by the imperialists after World War I were probably permanent and that they would never unite.

Nevertheless, the yearning to achieve, if not political unity, a common Arab destiny found expression everywhere. The tangible expression of that yearning was opposition to the state of Israel and espousal of the cause of the displaced Palestinians. Time and again, Arab governments, whether nationalist republics or monarchies (Jordan, Morocco, Saudi Arabia, and the Arab states of the Persian Gulf), sought to win the approval of their citizens and to voice their belief in a cause common to all Arabs by raising the war banner against Israel.

Zionism

Zionism, the movement to establish a distinctively Jewish state, began in Europe in the late 19th century. Like Arab and Turkish nationalism, Zionism was affected by other European nationalist movements and sought to weave a national identity out of feelings about religion (Judaism), language (Hebrew), and territory (the Holy Land). As members of a diverse movement, some Zionists put much more stress on one or another of these elements than did others, but all agreed on a fourth element that sets Zionism off from other nationalisms: anti-semitism—ingrained hatred and oppression of Jews.

Before 1800, the Jews of Europe had existed as a separate people distinguished from Christians by laws, customs, costume, religious observance, and, in many areas, language. The Jews of eastern Europe spoke Yiddish, a basically German language written in Hebrew letters. Many descendants of the Jews exiled from Spain in 1492 spoke Ladino, an archaic form of Spanish also written in Hebrew letters. European Christians, in general, disliked and distrusted the Jews, whom they stereotyped as greedy because of the involvement of some of them in money-lending. In fact, most Jews were poor and had few relations with people outside their communities. For hundreds of years, Christians had periodically expressed their animosity by expelling the Jews or embarking on murderous rampages, called pogroms, against them.

During the first half of the 19th century, France, Germany, and Austria "emancipated" the Jews by recognizing them as citizens. Oppression continued farther east in Poland, Lithuania, and Russia, but there too an "enlightenment" movement arose, stimulated by changes in Germany,

The creation of Israel and the numerous wars between Israel and its Arab neighbors have displaced thousands of Palestinians. Many of these people live in refugee camps set up by the U.N.

in which some Jewish leaders called upon their communities to abandon traditional costumes, learn to use the languages of the Christians, and participate in national affairs.

Many "emancipated" and "enlightened" Jews sought assimilation with the surrounding Christian society, some going so far as to change their religion. They believed that equality of citizenship was at hand and anti-semitism on the wane. It came as a profound blow, therefore, to discover, in the course of the Dreyfus Affair, a sensational court trial in France, that anti-semitic feelings in the most advanced of European countries were still deep and vicious. That discovery was the primary factor motivating Theodore Herzl, an Austrian journalist, to found the Zionist movement in 1896. He maintained that until the Jews had a homeland of their own, and learned to work the land and make it productive, they would never be respected by the European nations.

Most Zionists felt that their prospective homeland had to be in the Holy Land, then called Palestine, where the Jews of ancient times had had their kingdom, and where at least a handful of Jewish families had always lived. They therefore proceeded to buy land for Jewish settlements from the Arab landowners and seek the favor of the Ottoman Sultan who ruled it as part of his vast empire. The Arabs of Palestine feared and resented the expansion of Jewish settlements, particularly after the Jews insisted that only Jews could work on land owned by the Zionist organization. This restriction made sense in terms of Zionist ideology that called upon Jews to become "normal" by learning to work and love their own land; by contrast, the Arabs saw that the practice would result in more and more Arab tenant farmers being barred from land their families had worked for generations.

After gaining control of Palestine as a League of Nations "mandate" after World War I, Great Britain honored a wartime promise to foster the growth of the Jewish homeland. But it did not do so wholeheartedly because it feared the consequences of growing Arab discontent that might jeopardize the British political position in other Arab and Muslim countries. The balancing act between the Zionists and the Arabs was increasingly unsuccessful. Violent incidents punctuated the worsening Arab-Jewish confrontation and, in the 1930s, the Arabs of Palestine staged an armed rebellion against British policies. The suppression of that rebellion stifled the growth and development of a Palestinian Arab political community. By contrast, the Yishuv, as the Jewish community of Palestine was called, grew steadily stronger with its own governing institutions and underground military organizations. By this time, the dramatic resurgence of anti-semitism in Nazi Germany had added urgency to the Zionist mission.

Economically and psychologically depleted by World War II, and seeing no way of averting a showdown between the Arabs and the Jews in Palestine, Great Britain announced its plan to withdraw from Palestine and, in 1947, turned the problem over to the United Nations. The United Nations voted in favor of dividing the land into two states. When the British finally pulled out in 1948, the Zionists were ready to proclaim the state of Israel. The Palestinian Arabs had no effective leadership, however, and were unprepared to establish an Arab state alongside Israel. Fighting between the communities in Palestine escalated into war when the neighboring Arab states invaded.

The Arabs and Israelis have a number of seemingly irresolvable issues to solve before there can be a lasting peace in the Middle East. One nagging bone of contention is the continued Israeli occupation of, and the establishment of Jewish settlements in, the West Bank and the Gaza Strip.

During the yearlong conflict, Israel expanded its size beyond what the U.N. had authorized, 400,000 Palestinians became refugees either through flight from the fighting or through expulsion by local Israeli authorities, and most of the land remaining to the Palestinian Arabs was annexed by Jordan. In short, Zionism had realized its dream of an independent state, but at the cost of the dislocation and political disintegration of the Palestinian Arab community.

The U.S. and most European nations felt that the lopsided Zionist victory was justified by the newly revealed horror of the Holocaust, in which the Nazis had exterminated millions of Jews. The Arabs, however, saw this as a product of European guilt for which they were not at all responsible. Why, they argued, should the innocent Arabs of Palestine have to pay for the sins of the Nazis? Noting that many European governments had supported Zionism before World War II (and before the Holocaust), they saw Israel as an agent of European imperialism.

Although the sometimes forced, sometimes voluntary migration to Israel of large Jewish communities from Middle Eastern countries and the sporadic use of anti-semitic arguments by Israel's Arab adversaries tend to cloud the issue, one thing is certain: the wars fought between Israel and the Arabs in 1948, 1956, 1967, 1973, and 1982 have primarily reflected Arab feelings of nationalism vis-à-vis what they see as an expansive imperialist force and Israeli determination that Jews will never again allow themselves to be harmed or threatened without defending themselves.

In the course of the 1967 Six-Day War, Israel seized from Jordan the West Bank, part of the territory originally intended for a Palestinian state. This move raised the Israeli-Arab confrontation to a new level. On the Arab side, it prompted the development of a new and militant Palestinian leadership under the umbrella of the Palestine Liberation Organization (PLO); on the Israeli side, it offered to some Israeli politicians the hope that the captured land could be kept forever and become part of Israel. The U.N. Security Council voted in Resolution 242 that acquisition of land by force is inadmissible and that Israel should trade captured land for peace with its neighbors. This was actually done on the Egyptian front, where the Sinai Peninsula, also captured by Israel, was traded for a peace treaty. But the West Bank (and Gaza Strip) remain a bone of contention—some Israelis arguing that giving back Sinai was enough to satisfy the U.N. resolution—and a potential flashpoint for another Arab-Israeli war.

Oil

Successive American and European governments have shown much greater sympathy for the democratic political system and Western cultural values of Israel than for the bombastically anti-imperialist and often dictatorial Arab nationalist regimes. Nonetheless, the presence of vast oil reserves in the Middle East has made friendship with certain Middle Eastern states necessary. Following World War II, a vast expansion of petroleum use in Europe, North America, and, later, Japan led to increas-

The discovery in the Middle East of some of the world's largest oil deposits has vastly changed the political and economic relationship between western countries and Arab lands.

The oil-rich Middle East countries with small populations now rank among the wealthiest nations in the world. The more-densely populated Arab countries less blessed with oil resent the luxurious life-style and sometimes-haughty attitude assumed by their wealthy neighbors.

ing dependence upon Middle Eastern oil. The foreign-owned oil companies of Iran and Iraq had been producing oil before World War II. After the war, production was increased, and oil was soon flowing from Kuwait and Saudi Arabia, and later from Libya, Algeria, and the sheikdoms of the lower Persian Gulf.

Most of the oil lies beneath the desert sands in countries with very small populations. Iran, Iraq, and Algeria are the only producers with sizable populations; Turkey, Egypt, and Syria have little oil, as does Israel. Initially, the foreign oil companies that held concessions from the Middle Eastern governments controlled production and prices and paid as little as possible to the local governments. By the 1950s, however, some governments began to talk about taking over the companies operating in their territory, and some foreign countries began to pay larger royalties to prevent this nationalization. Through nationalization or negotiation or both, all of the oil-producing countries gradually acquired a much greater share of the oil profits. In 1960, they joined with several non-Middle Eastern countries to form the Organization of Petroleum Exporting Countries (OPEC).

During the 1973 Arab-Israeli war, the Arab oil producers attempted to use oil as a weapon by banning all sales to the United States and the Netherlands, two of Israel's friends. The embargo was neither successful nor long-lasting, but even the possibility that world oil supplies might fall short of demand had forced up the price. In 1974, OPEC forced the price up even higher, and an enormous amount of money from the oil-consuming countries began to flood into the oil-producing countries.

Countries with large populations, like Iran and Iraq, had plenty of useful things on which to spend their money; others, like Kuwait, Saudi Arabia, and the Persian Gulf sheikdoms, spent billions on lavish projects that enabled their tiny populations to live luxurious lives without much concern for efficiency or for the rapidly growing disparity between rich countries and poor countries. All of the newly rich countries spent huge amounts on weapons systems that they purchased from the West or from the Soviet Union.

Oil prices jumped again in 1979, when a revolution toppled the government of the Shah of Iran. Finally, in the 1980s, prices stabilized as the most powerful OPEC country, Saudi Arabia, came to the conclusion that moderate and stable oil prices were wiser in the long run than very high ones. To control prices, OPEC had to control supply; it did this by a series of quota agreements that set a limit to each member's production. Since this meant some states could not earn as much as they wanted to, constant pressure existed to exceed on the OPEC quotas; overall, however, the system worked fairly well.

Even after the worst fears of runaway oil prices died down, other oil-related problems persisted. One was temptation. Very wealthy states with populations too small to provide a significant army are traditionally easy prey for their neighbors. Another was inequality. As a non-Arab state with a large population, Iran was not expected to share its wealth with its neighbors. But within the country, the growing gap between the rich and the poor became a major cause of the revolution in 1979. Among the Arabs, on the other hand, the ideology of Arab nationalism suggested that the rich should help the poor. That they did, although the charity did not prevent every poor Arab from realizing that life in Saudi Arabia and Kuwait was steadily improving while their own standard of living was steadily getting worse.

Islam

Until the late 1970s, international involvement with the Middle East remained focused on the issues of Israel and the supply of oil. In the 1960s, Egypt's Nasser had been part of a global anti-imperialist, anti-colonialist leadership that, through support of Third World national liberation movements, was disrupting the European and American vision of world stability. Hence, Arab nationalism had been a matter of international and not just regional concern. But by the late 1970s, most national liberation movements had either succeeded or died, and Arab nationalism had become tarnished by the inability of most nationalist governments to provide better lives for their people. Ironically, with the exception of Iraq and Libya, the richest states were still monarchies. Iraq, ruled by the nationalistic Baath Party, sought to exercise greater clout in the Arab world by leading the other Arabs in ostracizing Egypt from the Arab community after Anwar Sadat made peace with Israel. But the Egyptian peace with Israel, by removing from contention the army of the largest Arab state, also crippled Arab hopes of defeating Israel militarily. Thus Arab nationalism declined in political importance, leaving the PLO the only nationalist force actively opposing Israel.

*The vast majority of Middle East residents adhere to Islam. Muslims perform a ritual prayer (*salat*) five times a day; during the prayer, they always face toward Mecca, the Islamic holy city.*

A strong fundamentalist movement has swept through the Islamic world. In Iran, an Islamic revolution led by Ayatollah Khomeini took control of the government in 1979.

The Islamic revolution in Iran, which burst upon the world in 1979, came as a complete surprise. In one sense, it should have been expected: since the 1950s, philosophers had been reinterpreting Islam as a revolutionary ideology against impious dictatorships and attacks on traditional culture by outside imperialists. By the late 1960s, a few astute observers of the Middle Eastern intellectual scene had recognized that the words of these philosophers were exciting enthusiastic responses among Muslim students all over the Islamic world. But at the time, most analyses of the nature of the modern world considered religion an obsolete force in politics that could safely be disregarded.

Outside of intellectual circles, therefore, the revolution in Iran came as a shock. The Shah's considerable strength led almost everyone to believe that he would use force to suppress the strikes and demonstrations that caused his downfall. Few people outside Iran could appreciate the immense popularity of the aged Ayatollah Khomeini, who led the revolution from exile in France by smuggling messages and instructions to his followers within Iran.

Khomeini's message, and that of Muslim activist leaders elsewhere, emphasized that even though the nationalist movement of the preceding decades had succeeded in eradicating the outward manifestations of imperialism—direct colonial rule, foreign military bases, ownership of the oil industry, etc.—it had culturally and intellectually succumbed to foreign influences. Secularism, a common theme of Turkish and Arab nationalist thinkers, was portrayed as an impious Western doctrine designed to undermine faith in Islam. Socialism, which was particularly popular among Arab nationalists like Nasser and the Baath Party, was seen, at least by some religious leaders, as a leftist attack on private property inspired either by European socialists or by the atheistic Soviet Union. And nationalism itself, which unquestionably derived from European thinking, was felt to foster unhealthy ethnic divisions and rivalries within the worldwide fraternal community of Islam, the Umma.

In this light, most ruling governments appeared to be disguised, and perhaps unconscious, agents—rather than opponents—of imperialism. The cure was to return to Islam as the primary source of law and public morality and to create new ways of instilling Islamic values in governments. Ayatollah Khomeini, although among the most conservative of leaders in social matters, was particularly creative. He proposed that a religious jurist—initially himself—be placed above the government to ensure, largely by retaining such powers as approving candidates for certain high offices and deciding on war and peace, that political leaders would not use their governing power to subvert Islam.

Internationally, the immediate effects of the Iranian revolution and the establishment of the Islamic Republic of Iran included a panicky run-up of oil prices and the severing of relations between Iran and the United States after President Carter admitted America's old friend, the fugitive Shah, to the U.S for medical treatment. Irate Iranians, who regarded the Shah as a criminal, responded by seizing the American embassy in Teheran and holding U.S. diplomats prisoner for 444 days. Within the Middle East, the revolution was immediately seen to have deeper significance. Publicly, officials in almost every country said that only Shiite Muslims were vulnerable to such revolutionary propaganda. Privately, leaders knew that many of their own Sunni Muslim citizens, including both university students and villagers newly moved to the city, were attracted to a new movement that promised to restore pride and a sense of identity in the face of increasingly dominant Western cultural images and social customs.

Unlike the Shah of Iran, most rulers elsewhere proved willing and able to suppress the Islamic movement by force. Many governments, particularly those of Egypt, Syria, and Iraq, resorted to arrests and executions to head off revolutions before they started. As the one example of a successful reassertion of Islam, Iran loomed as a frightening menace, a potential source of political and military support for Islamic movements elsewhere. When Iraq attacked Iran in September 1980, therefore, the real reason was not a dispute over a border treaty, as Iraq claimed, but fear that if the revolution was not blunted, its force would eventually lead to unrest and revolution both in Iraq and in other Arab countries.

The secular, socialist, Arab-nationalist regime led by Saddam Hussein fought Iran for eight years and did succeed in blunting the force of the Iranian revolution. By war's end, Iran was a severely weakened country beset by massive economic problems and largely isolated from the world community. Iraq, too, had suffered immense human and economic losses for little gain. Thus, it was particularly galling when other Arab states, such as Kuwait, asked for repayment of billions of dollars loaned to Iraq to finance the war. As Saddam Hussein saw it, if Iraq had sacrificed for eight years to win a victory that benefited all of the Arabs (except those in the Islamic movement), was it not unjust for a wealthy country like Kuwait to demand repayment?

Kuwait's refusal to forgive the debts of its powerful northern neighbor led directly to the Iraqi invasion on August 2, 1990. But while the ensuing Persian Gulf War distracted world attention from other Middle Eastern matters, the challenge represented by the Islamic Republic of Iran and by myriad Islamic movements in other countries persisted. Would the Arab nationalist regimes, some of which had evolved into brutal dictatorships, sooner or later, gradually or through revolution, succumb to the growing force of politicized Islam? Or would arrests and suppression suffice to stifle the challenge? Even the PLO found its leadership challenged within the West Bank and Gaza Strip by an Islamic movement called Hamas, which took a much more militant line against Israel. Hamas has helped sustain the *intifada,* a stone-throwing uprising in the occupied territories that has profoundly disturbed Israeli politics from December 1987 onward.

In the international arena there was the additional question of how the United States, the Soviet Union, and the European countries should react to the Islamic movement. The appeal of Islam as a moral, legal, and social system became increasingly felt among all classes of Middle Eastern society, despite the general feeling that Iran was an odious theocracy and that some Islamic activists, such as those who assassinated Anwar Sadat in 1982 and kidnapped various Americans and Europeans, resorted to terrorism. Interestingly, the king of Saudi Arabia, a staunch friend of the United States, presided over an Islamic social and legal system more severe and puritanical even than that in Iran. For the increasingly unstable Soviet Union, the Islamic movement posed yet another problem, since no one knew whether it might eventually attract the millions of Muslim citizens living in the southern republics of the U.S.S.R.

The Cold War

All of the disparate political movements and conflicts described in the preceding sections evolved in the world context of Cold War rivalry between the United States and the Soviet Union. Some of the very first conflicts between the superpowers after World War II took place in the Middle East. In 1946, the U.S.S.R. tried to avoid honoring a commitment to withdraw its troops from northeastern Iran. In 1947, President Truman enunciated an aid program to Greece and Turkey to combat the threat of communist subversion.

As the Cold War ends and we look back on its 45-year history, its profound influence is apparent. The Western European allies of the United States after World War II included the world's primary imperialist powers. The U.S. underwent wrenching bouts of conscience in deciding when to support liberation from colonial rule and when to rally to the side of the colonial power. The Soviet Union, meanwhile, was able to win the friendship of national liberation movements around the world because of its ideological opposition to imperialism as a late and obnoxious manifestation of capitalism. Many national liberation movements and newly independent countries reciprocated this friendship by adopting Communism as their ideology. Such was the case in the People's Democratic Republic of Yemen (South Yemen, now united with North Yemen in a single, non-communist republic). Others, such as Egypt, Syria, Iraq, Libya, and the PLO, welcomed Soviet military aid and political support and espoused some form of socialism; but they did not become part of the communist bloc. Soviet support was crucial to the early successes of Arab nationalism. American opposition to nationalist movements and regimes often had more to do with opposing Soviet influence than with an objective evaluation of the situation in regional terms.

Both the United States and the U.S.S.R. initially supported the creation of the state of Israel. The Soviets, however, found it easy to abandon

Israel and support the Arabs instead. Having suffered immense losses itself during World War II, the Soviet Union did not harbor guilt feelings about the Holocaust. Israel, despite its socialist economic system and the fact that most European Jewish immigrants came from Soviet bloc countries in eastern Europe, increasingly developed strong emotional, cultural, and economic ties with the democracies of the West. Moreover, the anti-semitic sentiments of czarist Russia did not disappear with the rise of the Soviet Union.

Soviet-American rivalry played a role, therefore, in every Arab-Israeli war after 1948. In 1956, the superpower rivals unexpectedly wound up on the same side when Soviet support for Nasser's Egypt coincided with U.S. anger that its allies, Britain, France, and Israel, had conspired to start a dangerous war without informing or consulting Washington. In subsequent wars, Israel depended increasingly on American weapons while its Arab adversaries were armed mostly by the Soviet Union. The superpowers competed with each other by selling or giving massive amounts of military equipment to the countries of the Middle East, making it

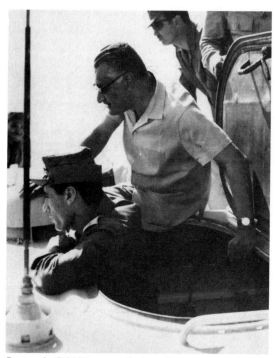

During the Cold War, many leaders of the Middle East turned to the Soviet Union as a means of offsetting American influence. Egypt's Nasser (shown at center above with Libya's Colonel Muammar Qadhafi) assumed a decidedly anti-American stance during his presidency.

the most heavily armed and, consequently, most explosive region in the world.

As the Soviet economy deteriorated in the late 1980s, however, and the U.S.S.R. became increasingly unstable politically, the superpower equation in the Middle East necessarily changed. Countries like Iraq and Syria worried that their main source of arms might soon dry up, causing them to become ever weaker vis-à-vis Israel in future years. Israel, on the other hand, began to hope that improving relations with the Soviet Union would permit the immigration to Israel of a million or more Soviet Jews. New Jewish citizens would help offset the substantially lower birthrate of the Jews versus that of their Arab neighbors in the occupied territories.

An unsettling implication of Israel's new hope, at least from the point of view of the U.S. and the Arabs, all of whom supported U.N. Security Council Resolution 242 calling upon Israel to trade the occupied land for peace with its neighbors, was that Israel might strive harder than ever to maintain permanent control of the occupied territories in order to have room for the Soviet immigrants. This possibility, combined with Arab fears of military weakness in the future, led many observers to fear that a new war in the region, either against Israel or implicitly involving Israel, might come sooner rather than later.

In the area of oil, the fact that the Soviet Union was self-sufficient in petroleum forestalled direct Soviet-American rivalry. Nevertheless, the

American desire to safeguard the oil resources of the Persian Gulf area and militarily protect friendly oil-producing governments seemed threatening to the Soviet Union because of the region's geographical proximity to the southern Soviet border. What resulted was a stalemate in which each superpower checked the other's attempts to establish a strong military presence or direct political control, but neither could prevent the other from selling or giving arms.in order to win friends. The result, both in the Persian Gulf and elsewhere in the region, was an arms race in which neither superpower could be sure that the friends it was arming would act as they wanted in time of crisis.

Islamic activism was the movement most immune from Cold War rivalries and therefore the one most likely to survive the end of the Cold War. Muslim activists regard both the West and the Soviet Union with disdain. "Neither East nor West" was a popular slogan in the Iranian revolution. Nevertheless, when the Soviet Union occupied Afghanistan in 1979 to support a revolutionary communist regime against an Afghan resistance deeply inspired by Islamic values, it became apparent even to the Muslim activists that the Cold War could not be avoided entirely. Despite American distaste for Islamic activism, the United States, in concert with Saudi Arabia and Pakistan, channeled massive military aid to the Afghan resistance. This meant that even though Iran and the United States remained passionately opposed to one another, they were fighting on the same side against the Soviet Union because Iran was supporting the Shiite resistance groups in Afghanistan.

It could be argued that insofar as the unpopular and unsuccessful war in Afghanistan discredited Leonid Brezhnev's hard-line application of Soviet power, the Islamic movement is responsible, to some extent, for the unraveling of the Soviet system. Similarly, Ayatollah Khomeini's

The United States found itself in the rather unusual position of supporting and channeling aid to an Islamic movement—the resistance group fighting the Soviet troops who were occupying Afghanistan.

The dissolution of the Soviet Union left the United States as the world's only superpower. Countries unfriendly to the U.S. suddenly found themselves without a source of military aid.

demonstration that the U.S. lacked the will or the power to free its diplomatic hostages helped undermine the presidency of Jimmy Carter and usher in the Reagan era. The implication of such arguments is not that the Islamic movement is uniquely powerful or dangerous, but rather that its growing force has introduced a new and unpredictable element in Middle Eastern politics. Analysts may well feel confident that they understand the complexities of Arab nationalist politics, Arab-Israeli rivalry, petroleum economics, and the Soviet-American relationship, both during and after the Cold War. But at the present time, no one can confidently predict the destiny of the Islamic movement—and no one can afford to ignore it.

The Persian Gulf War

Saddam Hussein's decision to invade Kuwait on August 2, 1990, represented a unique convergence of all of the trends discussed thus far. Though Saddam's rule of Iraq since 1979 had unquestionably been dictatorial and cruel, his decision to invade was far from being an irrational act. When Iraq's long war with Iran ended in 1988, Saddam, not unreasonably, declared victory. But he had few resources for rebuilding his country and compensating his people for their sufferings. Iraq's debts, mostly to Kuwait and Saudi Arabia, were heavy.

As a small country with great riches but only a tiny army, Kuwait had lived under the menacing shadow of its stronger neighbors ever since achieving independence in 1961. First Great Britain and then the United States had threatened Kuwait's enemies when necessary, but the fear remained. During the Iran-Iraq war, most Kuwaitis had viewed revolutionary Iran as their greatest threat. Once Iran had been defeated, however, Iraq resumed its status as most dangerous neighbor. Unwisely, the Emir of Kuwait decided to put obstacles in the way of Iraq's economic recovery. He adopted an oil policy that Iraq found unfriendly. He refused to grant Iraq control of some marshy islands that lay at the mouth of

Iraq's one usable accessway to the Persian Gulf (its other and more important accessway being disabled by war wreckage). And he refused to write off Iraq's war loans.

Saddam Hussein felt strongly that he had fought Iran on behalf of all Arab regimes and, indeed, by blunting the expansiveness of the Islamic revolution, he had done a great service for Arab nationalism. Therefore, he held the Kuwaitis to be ungrateful and mean-spirited. He countered their economic obstruction with military threats and the revival of a claim, dating to the earliest years of Iraqi independence, that Kuwait legally belonged to Iraq.

With its substantial oil reserves and bulging treasury, Kuwait was a rich prize well worth taking risks for. Though Saddam may have anticipated an international outcry over his invasion, he probably felt that it would eventually die down, leaving him not only free of his debts to Kuwait, but also in possession of that country's wealth besides. Since Iran was greatly weakened by the earlier war and sparsely populated Saudi Arabia was too weak militarily to intervene on Kuwait's behalf, the only real danger Saddam faced was from the United States.

The United States, of course, had not fought a significant war since its defeat in Vietnam. Furthermore, every Arab had a vivid memory of President Reagan's dispatch of U.S. forces to Lebanon in 1982. Supposedly part of a multinational peacekeeping force sent to help restore order after the Israeli invasion stalled on the southern outskirts of Beirut, the Americans had been goaded by terrorist threats and attacks into taking sides in Lebanon's simmering civil war. In response, a U.S. Marines barracks was blown up by a car bomb. Rather than committing U.S. forces further, President Reagan ordered a withdrawal. Thus an image had been created in the Arab world of the United States as a superpower that would bluster and threaten, but not actually fight.

In August 1990, Iraq invaded Kuwait and seemed poised to enter Saudi Arabia. This situation spurred Saudi Arabia to invite in American troops. Within months, a vast coalition of armed forces from both western and Arab countries had assembled in the region.

From the American point of view, however, the invasion of Kuwait offered a remarkable opportunity. The Cold War was over, and the global role of the U.S.—the one remaining superpower—had not yet been defined. A successful confrontation with Iraq, therefore, might help clarify the shape of the post-Cold War world. Even though the United States had become very friendly with Iraq toward the end of the Iran-Iraq war and had been willing to overlook the use of poison gas and threats against Israel in the interest of that friendship, so too was the United States friendly with Kuwait and Saudi Arabia.

It may never be known whether Saddam Hussein intended, sooner or later, to invade Saudi Arabia, but the possibility was sufficiently frightening to the Saudis and the United States for the former to invite in American troops, something Saudi Arabia had previously shied away from doing.

This was the first step in the mustering of a vast coalition of forces, both western and Arab, sworn to prevent further Iraqi aggression and liberate Kuwait.

Saddam Hussein countered the American force buildup by trying to link his occupation of Kuwait with Israel's occupation of the West Bank and Gaza Strip and Syria's occupation of a large part of Lebanon, a situation that began in 1976 when Syria intervened in Lebanon's civil war. By involving Israel, Saddam hoped to shame the Arabs into abandoning the coalition by pointing out that they were siding with Israel's great ally against fellow Arabs. The appeal of Arab nationalism directly confronted America's long-standing commitment to the safety of Israel. The Palestinians praised Saddam for standing up for their rights and remained on his side throughout the crisis.

The United States rejected Saddam's offer to withdraw from Kuwait in return for an Israeli withdrawal from the occupied territories. Several strategies were followed to keep the coalition from dissolving. First, some Arab countries were financially rewarded: the United States and Saudi Arabia relieved Egypt of over 7 billion dollars in debt. By contrast, Arabs siding with Saddam—Jordan, Yemen, and the PLO—suffered badly financially from a withdrawal of Saudi friendship. Secondly,

In the United Arab Emirates (above) and elsewhere in the Middle East, many people were outraged that Iraq's leader, Saddam Hussein, would order an invasion of Kuwait, a fellow Arab country. Saddam was widely disparaged in street demonstrations and by the media during the crisis.

the U.S. worked closely with the Soviet Union and other members of the United Nations Security Council to ensure that when and if fighting broke out, it would be under U.N. authorization. It was hoped that this would deflect the charge that the U.S. was acting as an imperialist power. And thirdly, diplomatic pressure was put on Israel to remain passive and not embarrass the Arabs in the coalition by trying to join the anti-Iraq coalition.

Since Saddam Hussein was convinced that the United States would not actually fight and President Bush was irreversibly committed to restoring the Kuwaiti government to power, the stage was set for war by the end of August. The following four-and-a-half months saw numerous unsuccessful attempts at mediation, including a futile final meeting in Geneva between Secretary of State James Baker and Iraqi Foreign Minister Tariq Aziz on January 9, 1991. But neither side weakened in its resolve.

On January 16 (January 17 in the Persian Gulf), Operation Desert Shield turned into Operation Desert Storm as the coalition army began an air attack on Iraqi strategic targets. Iraq responded with Scud missiles sent against Israel and Saudi Arabia, but Israel refused to play into Saddam's hands by retaliating. On February 24, the ground phase of the war began with a massive attack that punched through and outflanked the

Iraqi defensive positions in Kuwait. Through the course of the war, tens of thousands of Iraqis surrendered to coalition troops and became prisoners of war. By the time the war ended on February 27, as many as 100,000 Iraqi troops may have been killed versus only a handful of coalition casualties.

President Bush's decision to stop the offensive after Kuwait had been liberated preserved Saddam Hussein in power. At several points, the president had publicly urged the Iraqis to rebel against their leader. But when rebellions actually broke out among the Shiites of southern Iraq and the Kurds of northern Iraq, coalition forces stood by passively while the Iraqi army and police suppressed them. Only when the sufferings of Kurdish refugees were widely publicized was the United States shamed into taking up responsibility for refugee relief and safety.

It is still unclear why the United States decided to let Saddam Hussein remain in power and suppress his internal opposition. Was it fear that a successful Shiite rebellion would somehow help Shiite Iran regain influence in the region? Was it fear that a successful Kurdish rebellion would lead to a demand for a Kurdish state that would set a bad precedent in other parts of the Middle East? Was an understanding reached with the Soviet Union or some of the coalition allies that the offensive

The world was awed by the power and precision demonstrated by the Patriot missile (below) and other American weapons during the Persian Gulf War.

The Persian Gulf War ended shortly after the liberation of Kuwait. The United States emerged from the conflict as the predominant power in the Middle East.

would stop short of toppling the Iraqi government? Or was there a mixture of these and other motivations? However inexplicable Saddam Hussein's survival may be, the postwar world unquestionably saw the United States as the great victor and predominant power in the Middle East.

Shocked by the magnitude of the Iraqi defeat, the countries of the region waited to see what the United States would do with its newly acquired power. The first item on the American agenda was a diplomatic campaign to bring about a solution to the Arab-Israeli dispute via a peace conference. As that torturous process inched forward, eventually to result in the Madrid Peace Conference from October 30 to November 2, 1991, other less-publicized initiatives began. Negotiations were launched aimed at developing strategies to protect the small oil-producing countries of the Persian Gulf against future attacks. Other discussion concentrated on securing the release of American and European hostages held in Lebanon by Muslim activist groups sympathetic with Iran. Success in the latter endeavor—achieved by and large by the end of 1991—would presumably be followed, after a diplomatic interval, by an improvement in U.S.-Iranian relations. Finally, on the international scene, the United States attempted to portray the coalition victory and the successful wielding of authority by the United Nations Security Council as a model of how other post-Cold War crises might be managed. Thus all of the major strands of Middle East politics have come together in the calm after the Desert Storm. Now the world waits in hope to see what good might eventually come of the war's terrible death and destruction.

MID-EAST UPHEAVAL: A year-by-year overview

LEBANON	NORTH AFRICA	SYRIA	JORDAN AND THE PALESTINIANS	IRAQ

1943-1948

In 1943, **Lebanon** achieves independence from France. **National Pact** formalizes division of power among religious sects with Maronite Christians and Sunni Muslims taking highest offices.

In 1946, last French forces evacuate country.

Postwar **Morocco**, **Algeria**, and **Tunisia** are under French domination; Britain and France co-administer **Libya**.

◄ *North Africa served as a battleground during much of World War II. The war ultimately loosened the hold of the European colonial powers.*

In 1946, France evacuates **Syria**; independence of **Syria** recognized.

In 1948, **Syria** joins in attack on newly proclaimed state of **Israel**.

In 1947, Britain turns over problem of governing **Palestine** to the **United Nations**, which votes to partition the territory into two states, one Jewish, the other Arab.

In 1948, British withdraw; Transjordan joins in Arab attack on **Israel** on May 15. Palestinians are unable to form state or conduct significant military operations. Approximately 650,000 people become **Palestinian refugees**, some fleeing from embattled areas and others evicted by **Israel**. Jordanian army occupies territory west of the Jordan River (**West Bank**) designated part of intended Palestinian state in **U.N.** partition plan. Fortified border divides **Jerusalem**. On Dec. 1, **King Abdallah** renames country Hashemite Kingdom of **Jordan**.

▲ *Many Palestinians were displaced with the creation of Israel in 1948. Above, the U.N. supplies milk to young Palestinians in a refugee camp.*

1949

On July 20, armistice reached with **Israel**. Three successive military coups result in Colonel Adib Shishakli coming to power on Dec. 20. Shishakli suppresses all political parties.

1950-1951

On Dec. 24, 1951, **Libya** achieves independence. British install King Idris, leader of Sanusi religious organization.

On July 20, 1951, **King Abdallah** is assassinated. His son Talal succeeds to throne.

1952-1953

King Talal found mentally unfit to continue ruling. On Aug. 11, 1952, his son **Hussein** replaces him.

On Nov. 27, 1947, **U.N. General Assembly** votes for partition of British-controlled **Palestine** into two states, one Jewish, the other Arab.

On May 14, 1948, **Israel** declares its independence. Political and military organizations within the **Yishuv** take over duties of government. **David Ben Gurion** is first prime minister. Since it is evident that Palestinians are unprepared to claim the national rights granted in the **U.N.** resolution, neighboring Arab states attack **Israel** on May 15. In course of war, **Israel** expands beyond limits proposed by **U.N.**

On March 22,1945, **League of Arab States** (or **Arab League**) founded. Headquarters established in Cairo.

In 1948, **Egypt** launches war against newly declared state of **Israel**.

In 1946, **U.S.S.R.** challenges Iranian independence by remaining in occupation of northwest province. On May 9, Iranian diplomacy finally secures withdrawal.

In 1948, **ARAMCO (Arabian-American Oil Company)** formed to exploit newly discovered oil supplies in **Saudi Arabia**.

On March 12, 1947, the Truman Doctrine enacted to channel aid to Greece and **Turkey** to fight growing Communist threats. **U.S.** President **Harry Truman** exercises **U.S.** influence in getting **U.N. General Assembly** to vote for partition of **Palestine** on Nov. 27.

Egypt formed its own air force shortly after World War II, and limited the British military presence to the Suez Canal Zone.
▼

Armistices reached with **Egypt** (Feb. 24), **Lebanon** (March 7), **Jordan** (Apr. 3), and **Syria** (July 20). First parliament (Knesset) elected to write constitution; constitution remains unwritten.

Armistice with **Israel** reached on Feb. 24, 1949.

Mass immigration of Jews from Arab countries, particularly **Morocco**, **Yemen**, **Egypt**, and **Iraq**.

On March 29, 1951, nationalist **Mohammed Mossadegh** becomes prime minister.

On May 2, 1951, **Iran** nationalizes **Anglo-Iranian Oil Company**.

In 1950, **Turkey** joins NATO.

On July 23, 1952, military coup overthrows King Farouq. **Free Officers Corps** takes power with Revolutionary Command Council under nominal leadership of General Naguib.

On Aug. 16, 1953, **Mossadegh**'s growing power causes **Shah Mohammed Reza Pahlavi** to flee country. Within a few days, **U.S.** and British intelligence organizations help pro-Shah Iranian leaders overthrow **Mossadegh** and restore Shah.

On Nov. 9, 1953, **King Abd al-Aziz ibn Saud**, founder of Saudi kingdom, dies and is succeeded by son **Saud**.

LEBANON	NORTH AFRICA	SYRIA	JORDAN AND THE PALESTINIANS	IRAQ

1954-1955

On Nov. 1, 1954, **Algeria** begins its rebellion against French occupation.

◄ *In 1958, American troops arrived in Lebanon to help the country maintain political order.*

On Feb. 24, 1954, Shishakli ousted in coup; country returns to parliamentary rule. **Ba'th Party** actively participates in alliance with the military.

Syria becomes friendly with **U.S.S.R.**; military benefits from Soviet weapons.

British-sponsored **Baghdad Pact** seeks to make **Iraq** center of anti-Soviet military alliance.

1956

Tunisia and **Morocco** gain independence. Constitutional Neo-Destour Party rules in **Tunisia**. King Muhammad V rules in **Morocco**. Oil discovered in **Algeria**.

Syria sides with **Egypt** against **Israel** in Suez war. Cutting of oil pipeline from **Iraq** to the Mediterranean foreshadows later use of oil supplies as a weapon.

In 1961, British troops left ▶ Kuwait after helping the sheikdom resist an Iraqi threat of annexation.

1957-1958

Reformist army commander Fuad Shihab elected president. On July 15, 1958, **U.S.** Marines land in Beirut to forestall political deterioration.

On Feb. 1, 1958, **Syria** and **Egypt** join to form the **United Arab Republic** (**UAR**). **Ba'th Party** initially enthusiastic about cooperating with **Egypt**'s **Nasser**.

Attempt at union between **Iraq** and **Jordan**, whose kings are cousins, fails. On July 14, 1958, revolution overthrows monarchy. General Abd al-Karim Qasim comes to power. Qasim sees himself and **Iraq** as alternative center of **Arab nationalism**; Communist Party flourishes. **Iraq** friendly with **U.S.S.R.**

1959-1960

Oil discovered in **Libya**; exports begin in 1961.

1961

Algeria wins independence after grueling war. **National Liberation Front** (**FLN**) establishes single-party regime with Ahmed Ben Bella as president.

Muhammad V of **Morocco** dies; his son **Hassan II** succeeds to throne.

On Sept. 28, **Syria** secedes from **United Arab Republic**. New regime is anti-**Nasser**.

Syria and Egypt com- ▶ bined into one country, the United Arab Republic, in an agreement signed by Syrian president Shukri el Kuwatly and Egypt's Gamal Nasser.

	Gamal Abd al-Nasir (**Nasser**), real leader of the **Free Officers Corps**, replaces Naguib. On Oct. 26, 1954, assassination attempt against **Nasser** leads to suppression of **Muslim Brotherhood**. On Sept. 27, 1955, **Nasser** announces Egyptian purchase of arms from **U.S.S.R.**	On Oct. 11, 1955, **Iran** joins anti-Soviet **Baghdad Pact**.		On Feb. 24, 1955, agreement between **Iraq** and **Turkey** marks start of **Baghdad Pact**. Between Apr. and Oct., 1955, Britain, Pakistan, and **Iran** join pact.	1954-1955
On Oct. 29, seeking to curb cross-border raiding and gain maritime access to Red Sea, **Israel** invades **Egypt** in conspiracy with France and Great Britain. **Israel** occupies Sinai peninsula and **Gaza Strip** while French and British forces prevent Egyptian reinforcement by landing in canal zone, ostensibly to protect **Suez Canal**. On Dec. 22, Anglo-French force withdraws under **U.S.** and Soviet pressure.	On July 26, **Egypt** nationalizes **Suez Canal**. On Oct. 29, **Israel** attacks **Egypt** in Suez War. On Nov. 5, Britain and France land troops in canal zone, ostensibly to protect canal but actually to ensure Israeli military victory. **U.S.** and **U.S.S.R.** put pressure on France, **Israel**, and Britain to withdraw. **Nasser** seen by Arabs as hero for resisting invasion.			On Oct. 30, Britain and France, following plan prearranged with **Israel**, issue ultimatum to **Israel** and **Egypt** after **Israel** invades **Egypt**. On Nov. 5, Anglo-French force invades canal zone only to withdraw on Dec. 22 under **U.S.** and **U.S.S.R.** pressure. Britain and France humiliated and lose most of their influence in Middle East.	1956
	On Feb. 1, 1958, **Egypt** and **Syria** unite to form **United Arab Republic** (**UAR**). Measure appears to be first step toward unification of Arabs in fulfillment of goals of **Arab nationalism**.	*In 1954, huge crowds turned out to celebrate the one-year anniversary of the deposing of premier Mohammed Mossadegh and to honor the Shah and his father.*		In 1957, **U.N.** sends observers to monitor ceasefire on Egyptian-Israeli border. On July 15, 1958, **U.S.** Marines land in **Lebanon** to dampen growing political disturbances; they withdraw on Oct. 25.	1957-58
On March 7, 1959, last Israeli troops leave Sinai and **Gaza Strip**.			In 1960, **OPEC** (Organization of Petroleum Exporting Countries) founded in Baghdad. **Saudi Arabia** plays major role as largest exporter.		1959-1960
	In July, stringent socialist and nationalization decrees enacted in effort to create Arab Socialism. On Sept. 28, **Syria** secedes from UAR.		On July 19, **Kuwait** becomes independent of Great Britain. **Iraq** tries unsuccessfully to assert long-standing claim to **Kuwait**'s territory.		1961

25

1962-1963

◄ The "Black Feet" movement of poor French settlers in Algeria eventually evolved into a white terrorist organization opposed to the willingness of France to grant Algeria independence.

On March 8, 1963, **Ba'th Party** takes over government in coup. Attempts to form new union with **Egypt** or revolutionary **Iraq** fail.

Abd al-Karim Qasim killed in 1963 coup. **Ba'th Party** comes to power. Communist Party suppressed.

1964-1966

In 1965, coup in **Algeria** unseats Ahmed Ben Bella. Houari Boumedienne comes to power as head of **FLN**.

In 1964, military wing of **Ba'th Party** takes control.

On May 28, 1964, **Palestine Liberation Organization (PLO)** founded.

Palestinian guerrilla organization **al-Fatah** founded by **Yasir Arafat** in 1965.

In 1965, **Ba'th Party** ousted from power. Abd al-Sallam Arif, a pro-**Nasser** general, takes charge.

On April 13, 1966, General Abd al-Rahman Arif becomes president after his brother dies in helicopter crash.

1967

Egyptian prisoners-of-war are trucked away from the front while fresh Israeli troops arrive in the Sinai peninsula during the Six Day War in 1967.
▼

Six-Day War with **Israel** (June 5-10) leads to loss of Syrian territory of **Golan Heights**. Control by military elements in **Ba'th Party** increases.

Jordan badly defeated in **Six-Day War** (June 5-10). **Israel** occupies **West Bank** and **Gaza Strip**. On July 28, **Jerusalem** reunified and declared Israeli capital, a move rejected by many countries, including the **U.S.**

Kurds, shown here in ► traditional garb, have sought an independent homeland for many years.

1968

On March 21, 1968, **al-Fatah**'s role in helping repel Israeli attack on Jordanian town of Karameh enhances organization's prestige. National council of **PLO** taken over by **al-Fatah**.

On July 17, 1968, coup brings **Ba'th Party**, now led by General Ahmad Hasan al-Bakr and his lieutenant **Saddam Hussein**, back to power.

26

	In 1962, **Nasser** sends army to **Yemen** to intervene in civil war begun by military coup against the ruling Imam.	In July 1962, Shah announces series of reform measures (the White Revolution) as a means to counteract political opposition. In March, 1963, anti-Shah demonstrations are met by military force. Religious leader **Ayatollah Ruhollah Khomeini** is exiled in Nov. Two years later, **Khomeini** moves from **Turkey** to Shiite pilgrimage city of Najaf in **Iraq**.	Modernization encouraged in **Saudi Arabia** by Prince **Faisal**, the power behind the throne of brother **King Saud**. Imam Ahmad of **Yemen** dies and is succeeded on Sept. 19, 1962, by Imam Muhammad al-Badr. One week later, civil war is launched to overthrow Imam's rule. **Yemen Arab Republic** (YAR) is founded. Egyptian army intervenes to help republic fight tribes loyal to Imam.		**1962-1963**
State of military rule over Arabs in **Israel** ends in 1964.		*King Faisal ruled Saudi ▶ Arabia for 13 years. He began the long process of modernizing his kingdom.*	**King Saud** deposed by Saudi family. On Nov. 2, 1962, **Faisal** becomes king. 		**1964-1966**
On June 5, acting to preempt threatened attack by **Egypt**, **Israel** begins **Six-Day War** by destroying Egyptian and Syrian air force. Defeat of Egyptian army leaves **Israel** in control of **Gaza Strip**, Sinai peninsula, and east bank of **Suez Canal**. **Israel** takes **Golan Heights** from **Syria**. When **Jordan** enters war, **Israel** captures **West Bank** and east **Jerusalem**. On July 28, **Jerusalem** reunified and declared Israeli capital. Military settlements begin process of building Jewish population in formerly all-Arab areas.	On May 16, with much of his army still in **Yemen**, **Nasser** takes provocative action of asking **U.N.** armistice observers to withdraw from border with **Israel**. On June 5, **Israel** responds with preemptive air strikes to begin **Six-Day War**. **Egypt** loses **Gaza Strip** and Sinai peninsula to **Israel**. **Suez Canal** closed with Israeli troops entrenched on east bank.		On Nov. 30, British grant independence to People's Republic of South Yemen.	On Nov. 22, in aftermath of **Six-Day War**, **U.N. Security Council** issues **Resolution 242**, calling for Israeli withdrawal from occupied lands.	**1967**
		 ◀ *Following the Six Day War in 1967, the Suez Canal, which connects the Red and Mediterranean Seas, was closed. It did not reopen until 1973.*			**1968**

1969-1970

In Nov., 1969, Cairo agreements legitimize **PLO** political and military presence in **Lebanon**.

On Sept. 1, 1969, young army colonel **Muammar Qadhdhafi** overthrows King Idris and seizes power in **Libya**. He proposes union with **Egypt** but **Nasser** is reluctant to move too hastily after failure of union with **Syria**.

On Nov. 13, 1970, military faction of **Ba'th Party** under General **Hafiz al-Asad** achieves full control of government.

Al-Fatah controls executive committee of **PLO**. On Feb. 3, 1969, **Yasir Arafat** becomes **PLO** chairman.

In Sept. 1970, Black September clash between Palestinian guerrillas and Jordanian army leads to expulsion of **PLO** forces from **Jordan**.

On March 11, 1970, agreement is signed between **Ba'th Party** government and rebellious **Kurds** granting substantial Kurdish autonomy in north of country.

▲ *Colonel Muammar Qadhdhafi took over as Libya's leader in 1969. He has proved to be something of an erratic leader.*

1971

Two coup attempts in **Morocco** fail.

▲ *Smoke billows over the Jordanian capital of Amman as government forces rout Palestinian guerrillas during the Black September crisis in 1970.*

1972

Libya welcomes **U.S.S.R.** military support after **Anwar Sadat** evicts Soviet advisors from **Egypt**. **Libya** builds formidable army with Soviet weapons.

On Sept. 5, Palestinian guerrillas kill 11 members of Israeli olympic team in Munich in one of their most publicized acts of **terrorism**.

On Apr. 9, **U.S.S.R.-Iraq** Friendship Treaty is signed. Foreign-owned Iraq Petroleum Company nationalized.

Palestinian terrorists ▶ *killed 11 Israelis at the 1972 Olympics in Munich.*

1973

On Oct. 6, **Syria** and **Egypt** launch the **October War** against **Israel**.

Iraq sends troops to **Syria** to fight **Israel** in **October War**. Oil embargo and ensuing price increases multiply **Iraq**'s national income. Broad program of modernization begins.

◀ *Israeli troops bring in a Syrian soldier for questioning during the October War in 1973.*

1974

Habib Bourguiba, head of the Neo-Destour Party, elected president for life in **Tunisia**.

Syria regains part of **Golan Heights** from **Israel** in disengagement agreement arranged by **U.S.**

On Nov. 10, **Yasir Arafat** addresses **U.N. General Assembly**, marking major gain in **PLO** legitimacy.

Kurdish autonomy accords collapse on March 14, and **Kurds** renew rebellion.

28

The 1969-70 War of Attrition between **Egypt** and **Israel** marked by artillery fire across **Suez Canal** and Israeli air raids against Egyptian targets.

On Sept. 28, 1970, **Nasser** dies after trying to mediate resolution of conflict between **Jordan** and **PLO**. Vice President **Anwar Sadat** comes to power.

South Yemen state changes name to **People's Democratic Republic of Yemen** (PDRY) in 1969 as Communism emerges as dominant force.

Civil War in **Yemen Arab Republic** ends in 1970 with republicans in control.

On July 26, 1970, in Oman, British help Sultan Qabus ibn Said seize power from his father, Sultan Said b. Taimur.

In 1973, the Arab ban on oil exports to the U.S. and other countries caused gasoline shortages and skyrocketing prices.
▼

▲
U.S. Secretary of State Henry Kissinger, shown above meeting with Israel's Moshe Dayan, played a vital role in U.S. Middle East diplomacy in the early 1970s.

In Oct., Shah stages grandiose celebration of 2,500 years of monarchy at ancient capital of Persepolis. Emphasis on impressing world leaders causes bad feelings among population.

When British withdraw forces from **Persian Gulf**, **Iran** occupies militarily strategic islands in **Strait of Hormuz**, previously owned by Arab rulers of Dubay and Sharja.

British withdraw from **Persian Gulf**. **United Arab Emirates** founded as federation of seven small principalities. The oil-rich principality of Abu Dhabi enjoys the largest share of both land and wealth. **Qatar** and **Bahrain** remain separate countries.

On Sept. 5, Palestinian guerrillas kill 11 Israeli athletes at Munich olympics in highly publicized act of **terrorism**.

On July 18, **Sadat** orders expulsion of Soviet civilian and military advisors.

For the rest of the decade, a series of coups, assassinations, border wars, and failed unity agreements keep two Yemens in state of turmoil. Over a million Yemenis cross border to work in oil-rich **Saudi Arabia**.

On Oct. 16, **Egypt** launches surprise attack across **Suez Canal**. **October War** (also called Yom Kippur War and Ramadan War) comes as shock to **Israel** even though initial Egyptian advances are blunted and then reversed. On Oct. 23, both sides accept **U.N.** cease-fire resolution.

On Oct. 6, surprise attack by Egyptian forces overwhelms Israeli Bar Lev Line along **Suez Canal**. By time cease-fire is reached on Oct. 23, **Israel** has counterattacked across canal and surrounded major Egyptian army. Nevertheless, effective Egyptian fighting early in war restores Egyptian pride.

On Nov. 5, to support Arab struggle against **Israel**, **Saudi Arabia** leads **OAPEC** (Organization of Arab Petroleum Exporting Countries) in launching an embargo on oil shipments to allies of **Israel**. In four months, oil prices shoot from $2.90 to $11.65 per barrel.

U.S. resupplies **Israel** on eighth day of war with **Egypt**. From this time on, Israeli reliance on **U.S.** military aid becomes increasingly important. **U.S.** Secretary of State Henry Kissinger plays major role in arranging disengagement agreements between **Egypt** and **Israel** and **Syria** and **Israel**.

U.S. arranges first separation of forces agreement in Sinai peninsula. Israeli settlement of **West Bank** accelerates.

Iran plays leading role as **OPEC** hikes world oil prices drastically. Vast new wealth fuels modernization program.

World economics shocked by skyrocketing oil prices set by **OPEC**.

29

LEBANON	NORTH AFRICA	SYRIA	JORDAN AND THE PALESTINIANS	IRAQ

1975

On Apr. 13, civil war begins. Amal organization founded by religious leader Imam **Musa al Sadr** to represent interests of Shiites, now thought to be the largest segment of the population.

Spain withdraws from Spanish Sahara colony. **Morocco** claims possession of area and stages mass civilian Green March into what is now called Western Sahara. Polisario organization, with **Algeria**'s support, resists Moroccan occupation in prolonged guerrilla war.

Palestinian military presence in **Lebanon** contributes to tensions that cause outbreak of civil war on Apr. 13. Christian forces seek expulsion of **PLO**.

On March 7, agreement signed in **Algeria** by Shah of **Iran** and Vice President **Saddam Hussein**; **Iraq** accepts **Shatt al-Arab** river as the boundary between **Iran** and **Iraq** in return for **Iran** ceasing its support of the **Kurds**.

1976-1977

In 1976, **Syria** sends troops to **Lebanon** to forestall defeat of Christian forces, then changes side to protect **PLO** and Muslims.

Libyan-Egyptian border skirmishes in 1977 accentuate **Qadhdhafi**'s ambition to be a major figure in Arab politics.

In 1976, Syrian forces cross into **Lebanon** to intervene in civil war and remain in occupation of **Lebanon**'s interior.

1978

Musa al Sadr disappears on trip to **Libya**. Israeli troops move into heavily Shiite southern **Lebanon** and remain for three months.

Houari Boumedienne dies. Chedli Benjedid succeeds him as president of **Algeria**. Bread riots in **Morocco** and **Tunisia**.

Arab meeting in Baghdad declares steadfastness against **Israel** and isolates **Egypt** in punishment for **Sadat**'s agreeing to peace with **Israel**.

▲
Hafiz al-Asad has ruled Syria since 1970. Since Syria's loss of the Golan Heights, Asad has been careful to avoid direct conflict with Israel.

1979

Ahmad Hasan al-Bakr retires; **Saddam Hussein** becomes president.

Iraqi soldiers exalt before a bullet-pocked portrait of Ayatollah Khomeini during the early stages of the Iran-Iraq War.
▼

1980

▲
Palestinian refugees flee for cover during an air raid by Israeli warplanes over southern Lebanon.

Syria and **U.S.S.R.** sign treaty of cooperation and friendship. Syrian army suppresses **Muslim fundamentalist** uprising in Syrian city of Hama, destroying much of the city in the process.

Saddam Hussein initiates war against **Iran**, claiming that **Iran** failed to fulfill all terms of Algiers agreement. War is named **Saddam's Qadisiya,** after famous battle in Islamic history.

30

On Sept. 1, second Sinai separation of forces agreement is reached. As part of agreement **U.S.** agrees not to meet with **PLO**.

On Nov. 10, **U.N. General Assembly** resolution equating Zionism with racism signals growing power of anti-Israeli sentiment in **U.N.**

June 5, **Suez Canal** reopens after being closed for eight years.

On March 7, **Iran** signs Algiers agreement with **Iraq** promising to stop supporting Kurdish rebellion in **Iraq** in return for **Iraq** recognizing Iranian border claims along **Shatt al-Arab**. Iranian military intervention helps **Oman** bring an end to rebellion in Dhufar province.

On March 25, family member assassinates **King Faisal**. Brother Khalid takes over as king, but does not share **Faisal**'s high reputation for piety and morality.

Omani and Iranian armies finally suppress Dhufar rebellion encouraged by **PDRY**.

1975

In 1977, **Menachem Begin** becomes prime minister. **Likud** bloc replaces **Labor Party** as dominant force in Israeli government. Egyptian president **Anwar Sadat** speaks to Knesset in **Jerusalem**, inaugurating peace negotiations with **Israel**. Israeli military launches incursions into south **Lebanon**.

Increase in food prices sets off severe riots in Cairo. **Anwar Sadat** travels to **Jerusalem** to address the Knesset in gesture of peace. Economic and political liberalization (**Infitah**) slowly getting under way.

The establishment of ▶ Jewish settlements in the Israeli-occupied territories has created much discord between Israel and its Arab neighbors.

1976-1977

U.S. President **Jimmy Carter** brings **Menachem Begin** and **Anwar Sadat** to **Camp David** and persuades them to agree on peace accords.

Sadat meets with **Menachem Begin** and **Jimmy Carter** at **Camp David** to discuss peace.

Anti-shah demonstrations and strikes. A climax is reached on Sept. 8 when hundreds of unarmed civilians are reported dead after attack by army in Tehran's Jaleh Square. In Oct., **Iraq** expels **Ayatollah Khomeini**, who takes up residence in France. From there he encourages revolution with speeches smuggled into **Iran**.

President **Jimmy Carter** persuades **Anwar Sadat** and **Menachem Begin** to sign **Camp David Accords**, providing for peace between **Egypt** and **Israel** and forseeing eventual autonomy for Palestinians in **West Bank** and **Gaza Strip**.

1978

In 1978, Egypt's Anwar Sadat (left) and Israel's Menachem Begin (right) signed the Camp David Accords, providing for peace between the two countries.

The **Camp David Accords** peace treaty between **Egypt** and **Israel** is signed.

Camp David Accords with **Israel** lead to Egyptian expulsion from **Arab League** and isolation in the Arab world.

On Jan. 16, **Shah Mohammed Reza Pahlavi** flees **Iran**. **Ayatollah Khomeini** returns in triumph. Interim government is headed by Mehdi Bazargan. **U.S.** embassy seized by student radicals; diplomats held for 444 days in **hostage crisis** that destroys relations between **U.S.** and Islamic Republic.

Muslim fundamentalist group attacks mosque in Mecca, **Saudi Arabia**, **Islam**'s holiest city, trying to overthrow what they see as a sinful Saudi monarchy. French troops help suppress revolt.

Shah of **Iran** admitted to **U.S.** for treatment of cancer. Iranian anger at favorable treatment of deposed shah leads to takeover of American embassy in Tehran and **hostage crisis**.

1979

Golan Law makes **Golan Heights** part of **Israel**.

Constitution of Islamic Republic of **Iran** approved in plebiscite. Abolhassan Banisadr elected president. **U.S.** attempt to free hostages by a military raid fails.

U.S. effort to rescue hostages in Tehran fails.

War begins between **Iraq** and **Iran**.

1980

Israel bombs Osirak nuclear reactor, temporarily thwarting Iraqi plans to build nuclear weapons.

◀ *Members of the Palestinian Liberation Army evacuated Lebanon for Cyprus in 1982.*

1981

1982

Israel invades and occupies **Lebanon** south of Beirut; **PLO** evacuates country; Christian **Phalange (Kata'ib)** militia, with tacit permission of Israeli occupiers, kill several hundred people in Palestinian refugee camps on outskirts of Beirut.

Newly elected president Bashir Gremayel, leader of the **Phalange (Kata'ib)** political party, is assassinated. His brother Amin succeeds him.

Syrian air force badly defeated by **Israel** in air battle. Thereafter **Syria** is careful not to confront **Israel** directly in **Lebanon**.

Israel invades **Lebanon** with objective of destroying **PLO**. Palestinians initially overwhelmed but fight more effectively as Israelis near Beirut. Palestinians in Sabra and Shatila refugee camps on outskirts of Beirut massacred by Lebanese Christian forces. **PLO** evacuates **Lebanon**, moving headquarters to Tunis.

1983

U.S. president **Ronald Reagan** indicates that **Libya** is a particularly dangerous source of **terrorism.**

1984

Multinational force withdraws after attacks that include bombing of **U.S.** Marine barracks. Israeli forces withdraw but retain control of security zone in south through South Lebanon Army, a Lebanese Christian force paid and supplied by **Israel**.

In one of the most notorious acts of terrorism, the cruise ▶ ship Achille Lauro *was seized and one of its American passengers killed. At right, American Marilyn Klinghoffer, widow of the murdered passenger, disembarks after the crisis ended.*

1985-1986

In 1985, **U.S.** journalist Terry Anderson taken hostage in wave of **terrorism** carried out by radical Shiite groups.

In Apr., 1986, **U.S.** bombs Tripoli, **Libya**'s capital, as punishment for alleged Libyan complicity in terrorist incident in Germany. **Qadhdhafi**'s young daughter killed in attack. Evidence against **Libya** never publicly revealed.

In 1986, U.S. warplanes ▶ struck the Libyan capital of Tripoli in retaliation for alleged Libyan-sponsored terrorism.

Israeli warplanes bomb Osirak nuclear reactor.

Sadat assassinated by **Muslim fundamentalist** group. **Husni Mubarak** succeeds him.

Falling Iraqi and Iranian oil exports caused by war send up price of oil from $23 to $34 per barrel.

Encouraged by revolutionary **Iran**, **Muslim fundamentalists** stage unsuccessful coup against ruler of **Bahrain**.

Gulf Cooperation Council formed to bring **Persian Gulf** states closer together economically and militarily. All Gulf states join except **Iran** and **Iraq**.

Israel invades **Lebanon** in effort to crush **PLO**. As invasion bogs down and Lebanese civilian casualties mount, **Operation Peace in Galilee** loses popularity at home and abroad. **Israel** widely held responsible for permitting Christian Lebanese militia to kill Palestinians in refugee camps in Israeli-occupied territory.

▲ *In 1981, Anwar Sadat was assassinated by Muslim fundamentalists while reviewing a military parade.*

King Khalid dies and is succeeded by **King Fahd ibn Abd al-Aziz**. For first time **OPEC** agrees to oil production quotas as supply begins to outstrip demand, despite panic reaction to **Iran-Iraq War.**

U.S. Marines land in **Lebanon** as part of multinational peacekeeping force.

In aftermath of unpopular war, **Menachem Begin** resigns as prime minister and retires from politics. New **Likud** leader **Yitzhak Shamir** succeeds him.

▲ *In 1983, the U.S. suffered heavy losses when its Marine barracks in Lebanon was bombed.*

Unity government formed in 1985 between **Likud**, led by Shamir, and **Labor Party**, led by Shimon Peres. Israeli forces withdraw from **Lebanon**.

Israel stepped up security ▶ *in the occupied territories after several incidents in which Jewish citizens were stabbed to death.*

Oil prices collapse in 1986. Income of Arab oil states drops, putting development plans in jeopardy.

Muslim fundamentalists attempt assassination of **Shaikh Jaber al-Sabah**, ruler of **Kuwait**. Shaikh Jaber orders parliament closed and elections suspended until further notice.

1981

1982

1983

1984

1985-1986

33

LEBANON	NORTH AFRICA	SYRIA	JORDAN AND THE PALESTINIANS	IRAQ

1987

Christian leader Michel Aoun held out against Syrian forces in Lebanon for several months before taking refuge in the French embassy.
▼

Habib Bourguiba, now erratic in his old age, removed from power in **Tunisia**. New president Zein al-Abidin Ben Ali promises political liberalization and begins conciliation with **Muslim fundamentalists**.

Palestinian uprising (**Intifada**) begins on **West Bank** and in **Gaza Strip**.

Iraqi warplane attacks *USS Stark* on patrol in **Persian Gulf**. U.S. accepts explanation that attack was accidental, but increases military power in **Persian Gulf**, thus becoming involved in **Iran-Iraq war**.

1988

Serious bread riots in **Algeria**.

▲
Young Palestinians, using whatever weapons available to them, harass Israeli troops in the early days of the intifada.

PLO accepts **United Nations resolutions 242 and 338**, formally recognizing **Israel**'s right to exist. State of **Palestine** proclaimed. **King Hussein** renounces Jordanian claim to **West Bank**. **U.S.** initiates talks with **PLO** on the condition that **PLO** live up to promise to abandon **terrorism**.

In March, Iraqi army uses poison gas against Kurdish Iraqi citizens in town of Halabja. Incident brings broad condemnation as evidence appears irrefutable. In Aug., as **U.S.** support for **Iraq** in war becomes increasingly apparent. **Iran** accepts **U.N.** cease-fire resolution and war ends.

1989

Civil war ends. Agreement reached at Taif, **Saudi Arabia**, provides for reconciliation among the political factions and paves way for reestablishment of centralized government. Last remaining barrier, the Christian commander of Lebanese Army General Michel Aoun, occupies presidential palace and refuses to recognize new government.

◄ *In 1989, President and Mrs. Bush entertained King Hussein of Jordan and his American-born wife, Queen Noor, at a White House state dinner.*

Jan.-June 1990

In June, **FLN** loses municipal elections to **Muslim fundamentalists** in **Algeria**. **FLN** monopoly on power seriously eroded.

U.S. breaks off talks with **PLO**, charging **PLO** complicity in new guerrilla attack on **Israel**.

Saddam Hussein warns at a May Arab summit meeting that his country is being strangled by "its brothers." Primary complaint is against **Kuwait** for not forgiving loans made to help **Iraq** fight **Iran** and for adopting oil policies hostile to **Iraq**'s interests.

July 1990

On July 17, **Saddam Hussein** warns **Kuwait** and **United Arab Emirates** to revise their oil policies.

34

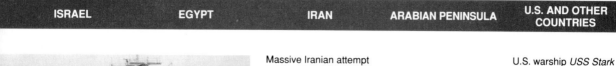

Massive Iranian attempt to take city of Basra fails, the turning point of the **Iran-Iraq War**.

◄ *In 1987, 37 American sailors were killed when the* USS Stark *was struck by an Iraqi Exocet missile during the Iran-Iraq War.*

U.S. warship *USS Stark* attacked by Iraqi plane in **Persian Gulf**. President **Reagan** accepts explanation that attack is accidental but orders build-up of military naval strength in area. **U.N. Security Council** passes cease-fire resolution unacceptable to **Iran**. **Iraq** accepts resolution while **Iran** presses for modifications.

1987

Palestinian uprising in **Gaza Strip** and on **West Bank (Intifada)** begins.

Egypt readmitted to **Arab League**.

Ayatollah Khomeini agrees to accept **U.N.** cease-fire resolution. War ends with **Iraq** holding upper hand.

Agreement to reflag Kuwaiti ships as American vessels draws the **U.S.** more deeply into war on Iraqi side. Exhausted militarily and convinced the **U.S.** is siding with **Iraq**, **Iran** accepts unmodified cease-fire resolution.

1988

▲ *Hundreds of thousands of mourners attended the funeral of Iran's Ayatollah Khomeini*

Massive immigration of Jews from **U.S.S.R.** begins.

◄ *Beginning in 1989, thousands of immigrants from the Soviet Union began arriving in Israel.*

Khomeini dies. **Ayatollah Khamenei** succeeds to his position as Revolutionary Guide and **Vali Faqih** (Governing Religious Jurist). Real power increasingly centers on President **Hashemi Rafsanjani**, a pragmatist; strength of religious radicals begins to ebb.

Breakup of Soviet empire in Eastern Europe and turmoil within the **U.S.S.R.** itself worries Middle Eastern countries dependent on Soviet arms.

1989

On May 22, **YAR** and **PDRY** finally unite in single Republic of **Yemen** as new-found oil resources bring promise of rapid economic development.

Jan.-June 1990

On July 24, **Husni Mubarak** confers with **Saddam Hussein** in Baghdad, reports **Iraq** will not invade **Kuwait**.

On July 17, **Kuwait** and **United Arab Emirates** warned by **Saddam Hussein** to revise their oil policies.

On July 24, **UAE** and **U.S.** stage joint military exercises in hopes of deterring Iraqi aggression.

On July 25, in interview with **Saddam Hussein**, **U.S.** ambassador April Glaspie indicates that **U.S.** does not have a fixed position on **Iraq**'s dispute with **Kuwait**.

July 1990

35

On Aug. 3, **Arab League** meeting in Tunis condemns **Iraq**'s invasion of **Kuwait**. 6 of the 20 members abstain.

On Aug. 10, **Arab League** votes to send troops to **Saudi Arabia** to oppose Iraqi invasion. Only 12 of the 20 members support resolution; **Libya** and **PLO** support Iraqi position, while others abstain.

On Aug. 11, contingent of Moroccan troops arrives in **Saudi Arabia**.

On Aug. 20, **Libya** backs away from support for **Saddam Hussein** by condemning the taking of foreign hostages.

On August 2, 1990, Iraqi troops poured into Kuwait and immediately seized the capital city (below). The Kuwaiti ruler, Emir Jaber al-Sabah (below right), fled the country for safety in Saudi Arabia. Citizens of western countries caught in Kuwait or Iraq at the time of the invasion were not permitted to return home for several months. Saddam Hussein appeared on national television with several of the detained foreigners, including a young British boy (right).

On Aug. 3, **Syria** joins in **Arab League** condemnation of **Iraq**. Though both countries are ruled by branches of **Ba'th Party**, they are intense rivals with a long history of intrigues against each other.

On Aug. 11, **Syria** says it will send troops to **Saudi Arabia** to join coalition.

On Aug. 3, **Saddam Hussein** tells **King Hussein** that he is willing to withdraw from **Kuwait** if he is not condemned by **Arab League**. **Arab League**, however, has already voted its condemnation.

On Aug. 16, after meeting with President **Bush**, **King Hussein** says he will honor **U.N.** embargo on trade with **Iraq** even though **Jordan** is the most important land route to **Iraq**. Questions about possible Jordanian violations of embargo arise repeatedly throughout crisis.

On Aug. 1, negotiations between **Iraq** and **Kuwait** collapse when Iraqis insist on total forgiveness of war debt.

On Aug. 2, 80,000 troops of **Iraq**'s elite Republican Guard cross into **Kuwait** at 2:00 A.M. and quickly take control of entire country. **Iraq** announces that Provisional Free Kuwait Government run by "young revolutionaries" invited invasion.

On Aug. 4, Baghdad announces formation of new military government in **Kuwait**.

On Aug. 5, **Iraq** claims it is withdrawing troops from **Kuwait**.

On Aug. 6, **Saddam Hussein** informs **U.S.** diplomat that **Kuwait** rightly belongs to **Iraq** and warns the **U.S.** not to intervene.

On Aug. 8, **Iraq** annexes **Kuwait**.

On Aug. 10, **Iraq** sets deadline for closing all foreign embassies in **Kuwait**.

On Aug. 12, **Saddam Hussein** suggests he might agree to withdraw from **Kuwait** if **Israel** withdraws from **West Bank** and **Gaza Strip**. Possibility of "linkage" is discussed throughout crisis but consistently rejected by **Israel** and the **U.S.**

On Aug. 17, **Saddam Hussein** announces he will use foreigners trapped in **Iraq** as "human shields" to protect military and strategic targets.

Iraqi TV Taped Broadcast

36

On Aug. 2, **Egypt** puts its airborne brigade on active standby as Iraqi forces move into **Kuwait**.

On Aug. 11, first Egyptian troops arrive in **Saudi Arabia**.

On Aug. 9, Iranian foreign minister says **Iran** will not tolerate changes in the political geography of **Persian Gulf**.

On Aug. 16, **Iran** agrees to honor sanctions against **Iraq**.

On Aug. 1, negotiations between **Kuwait** and **Iraq** break down. **Kuwait** insists on repayment of multibillion dollar war debt.

On Aug. 2, Kuwaiti Emir **Jaber al-Sabah** and Crown Prince Saad al-Sabah flee country as **Iraq** invades. Hundreds of thousands of Kuwaitis ultimately find their way into exile.

On Aug. 3, as **Saudi Arabia** braces for possible Iraqi invasion, **King Fahd** is reassured by President **Bush** that **U.S.** will stand by its ally.

On Aug. 5, after some hesitation, **Saudi Arabia** agrees to receive **U.S.** troops.

On Aug. 7, **U.S.** airlifts troops to **Saudi Arabia**. **Gulf Cooperation Council** calls for Iraqi withdrawal.

On Aug. 9, **Saudi Arabia's King Fahd** publicly condemns Iraqi invasion and says that **U.S.** and British troops will stay on Saudi soil only as long as emergency lasts.

On Aug. 11, Egyptian and Moroccan troops land in **Saudi Arabia**, adding Arab legitimacy to growing anti-**Iraq** coalition.

On Aug. 18, **Saudi Arabia** increases oil production to help compensate for loss of supply caused by **U.N.** embargo on Iraqi and Kuwaiti oil.

On Aug. 29, **OPEC** agrees to raise production to prevent possible world oil shortage.

On Aug. 3, **U.N. Security Council** votes 14-0 with **Yemen** abstaining to condemn invasion of **Kuwait** and demand Iraqi withdrawal. **U.S.** president **Bush** telephones **Saudi Arabia's King Fahd** to assure him of **U.S.** support in case of Iraqi invasion.

On Aug. 4, European Community slaps embargo on oil from **Iraq**.

On Aug. 6, **U.N. Security Council** vote imposes trade and financial boycott on **Iraq**. **Yemen** and Cuba abstain.

On Aug. 7, **U.S.** dispatches troops to **Saudi Arabia**. Troop commitment rapidly increases to 240,000 by mid-October. **Turkey** stops shipping Iraqi oil received via pipeline from **Iraq**.

On Aug. 8, making clear absolute **U.S.** opposition to Iraqi invasion, President **Bush** says "a line has been drawn in the sand."

On Aug. 12, **U.S.** Navy ordered to block all Iraqi oil shipments.

On Aug. 17, first call-up of **U.S.** military reserves.

On Aug. 24, **U.S.** keeps embassy open in **Kuwait** in defiance of Iraqi order. Iraqi troops cut off supplies from embassy personnel.

On Aug. 25, **U.N. Security Council** authorizes stopping Iraqi shipping on high seas to enforce embargo. **Yemen** and Cuba abstain.

In an early sign that the Cold War had ended, the Soviet ambassador to the United Nations voted with the U.S. and British ambassadors to impose sanctions on Iraq.

Operation Desert Shield began within a few days of the invasion of Kuwait. American troops poured into Saudi Arabia for many months before the actual war began.

Sept. 1990

On Sept. 10, **Arab League** moves from Tunis back to Cairo, its headquarters prior to the expulsion of **Egypt** after it made peace with **Israel**.

On Sept. 17, conference in Amman, **Jordan**, attended largely by members of Palestinian guerrilla oranizations and Jordanians, resolves to "strike against American interests everywhere." Even though no significant terrorist threat develops, fear of **terrorism** is widely felt.

On Sept. 21, **King Hussein** admits that his efforts to mediate a solution to the crisis by taking a neutral position have been a failure.

On Sept. 21, **Saddam Hussein** tells Iraqi people to prepare for "mother of all battles."

▲
PLO leader Yasir Arafat (left) met with Jordan's King Hussein to discuss the Gulf crisis. Neither leader supported the Allied cause.

Oct. 1990

On Oct. 13, Syrian army defeats General Michel Aoun's forces in **Lebanon**, removing last obstacle to Syrian-sponsored resolution of Lebanese civil war. Syrian participation in anti-Saddam coalition believed important in persuading **U.S.** to accept this expansion of Syrian power in **Lebanon**.

On Oct. 7, **Jordan** orders stringent austerity measures in the face of cut-off of oil from **Saudi Arabia**, economic deterioration caused by trade embargo, and the burden of caring for refugees from **Iraq**.

On Oct. 17, suspension of Saudi Arabian financial support to **PLO** revealed.

On Oct. 5, at **U.N. General Assembly**, **Iraq** claims that the **U.S.** and its allies are starting new wave of imperialism.

Nov. 1990

On Nov. 4, new Syrian troops arrive in **Saudi Arabia** to reinforce contingent already contributed to coalition.

On Nov. 16, **Iraq** accedes to Iranian demands in settling outstanding problems left from **Iran-Iraq War**.

On Nov. 19, **Iraq** sends more troops to **Kuwait**.

◀ *Beirut residents began the long process of cleaning up their city as the prolonged civil war finally ended.*

On Sept. 4, responding to **Egypt**'s strong condemnation of **Iraq** and willingness to work with the **U.S.** in reversing aggression, President **Bush** announces forgiveness of $7 billion in Egyptian debts.

On Sept. 10, twelve members of **Arab League** supporting coalition against **Saddam Hussein** vote to return League's headquarters to Cairo.

On Sept. 10, **Iran** and **Iraq** resume diplomatic relations. Given Iranian animosity toward the **U.S.**, the possibility of **Iran** helping **Iraq** looms throughout crisis, even though Iranian people hate **Saddam Hussein** from previous war.

On Sept. 17, **Saudi Arabia** restores relations with **U.S.S.R.** broken off in 1938.

On Sept. 19, stung by Yemeni support for **Iraq**, **Saudi Arabia** expels Yemeni diplomats and gives hundreds of thousands of Yemenis one month to leave country.

On Sept 9, at summit meeting in Helsinki, Presidents **Bush** and Gorbachev pledge to reverse Iraqi aggression.

On Sept. 25, **U.N. Security Council** imposes embargo on air connections with **Iraq**. Debate continues over whether sanctions are working and what "working" means if **Iraq** remains in occupation of **Kuwait**.

On Oct. 8, Israeli police kill 21 Palestinians outside of mosque in **Jerusalem**. Iraqi efforts to link its withdrawal from **Kuwait** to withdrawal by **Israel** from **West Bank** and **Gaza Strip** excites broad condemnation.

On Oct. 9, **Saddam Hussein** threatens **Israel**.

On Oct. 13, **Kuwait**'s Crown Prince Saad suggests that the Kuwaiti parliament, suspended in 1986, might be restored once **Iraq** withdraws.

On Oct. 21, some 350,000 Yemeni workers are reported to have left **Saudi Arabia**. Number eventually approaches one million.

On Oct. 25, President **Bush** adds 100,000 more troops to 240,000 already committed. Iraqi forces in **Kuwait** estimated at 500,000.

On Oct. 29, Secretary of State Baker says **U.S.** "will not rule out a possible use of force if **Iraq** continues to occupy **Kuwait**." General Norman Schwartzkopf's plan for a mid-January war is secretly presented to White House. President **Bush** decides to pursue war option and to seek a **U.N.** vote giving him suitable authorization.

On Nov. 16, agreement between **Iran** and **Iraq** settles outstanding problems in **Iran**'s favor.

On Nov. 3, Saudi Arabian oil production reaches highest level in 9 years.

On Nov. 8, President **Bush** commits 150,000 more troops to **Saudi Arabia**.

On Nov. 22, Great Britain's force commitment slated to be 30,000 by year's end.

On Nov. 29, **U.N. Security Council** votes resolution 678 authorizing use of force if **Iraq** does not withdraw from **Kuwait** by Jan. 15; **Yemen** and Cuba vote no; China abstains.

On Nov. 30, President **Bush** invites Iraqi Foreign Minister Tariq Aziz to Washington and says he will send **U.S.** Secretary of State Baker to Baghdad.

◄ *American and allied troops spent the fall of 1990 drilling, setting up bases, and preparing for the inevitable war.*

39

Dec. 1990

On Dec. 29, Iraqi opposition groups in exile meet in Beirut to seek common ground in case **Saddam Hussein** falls from power.

On Dec. 13, **Algeria**'s President Chedli Benjadid attempts mediation with **Saddam Hussein** in Baghdad. Attempt fails.

◄ *Jordan was flooded with refugees from Iraq and occupied Kuwait. Queen Noor played an important role in seeking aid for the refugees.*

On Dec. 1, **Iraq** accepts **U.S.** proposal to enter into talks via an exchange of visits by foreign ministers.

On Dec. 6, **Saddam Hussein** offers to free all foreign hostages by Christmas.

On Dec. 22, **Saddam Hussein** warns that if war comes, Tel Aviv will be first target, and hints at use of guided missiles.

Jan. 1991

On Jan. 30, Palestinian-Israeli fighting erupts in southern **Lebanon** in response to Palestinian rocket attack. Fears that a second front may draw **Israel** into the war prove unfounded.

Operation Desert Shield became Operation Desert Storm on January 17, when the air phase of the Persian Gulf war went ahead. The allies established almost immediate air supremacy.
▼

On Jan. 1, new Jordanian cabinet includes **Muslim fundamentalists**.

On Jan. 14, after meeting with **Saddam Hussein**, **Yasir Arafat** says "**Palestine** and **Iraq** stand in one trench to regain Arab rights."

On Jan. 4, **Iraq** agrees to meeting of foreign ministers in Geneva on Jan. 9. Meeting ends in deadlock.

On Jan 12, last foreign diplomats leave Baghdad.

On Jan. 17, air war begins; **Iraq** fires Scud missiles at **Israel** and **Saudi Arabia**.

On Jan. 22, more missiles fired at **Israel**. Iraqi strategy is to provoke Israeli retaliation that will make Arab members of coalition reluctant to continue fighting as *de facto* allies of **Israel**. Attacks on **Israel** increase **Saddam Hussein**'s popularity among Palestinians and Jordanians as well as Arabs elsewhere.

On Dec. 1, **Saudi Arabia** cancels $4 billion in Egyptian debt.

On Dec. 31, **Iran** pledges to remain neutral if war comes.

On Dec. 19, Amnesty International reports large scale torture and killing by Iraqi forces occupying **Kuwait**.

On Dec. 25, **Gulf Cooperation Council** summit conference demands unconditional Iraqi withdrawal.

On Dec. 1, President of **Turkey**, Turgut Özal, proposes Allied coalition use Turkish airbase at Incirlik.

On Dec. 9, **U.S.** denounces **Saddam Hussein**'s proposal that **U.S.** Secretary of State Baker visit Baghdad only three days before expiration of **U.N.** deadline as a delaying tactic.

On Dec. 11, last Americans leave **Iraq**.

On Dec. 13, **U.S.** embassy in **Kuwait** is evacuated.

◄ *The threat of chemical attack led Israel to provide its citizens with gas masks.*

On Jan. 17, Scud missile hits **Israel** as air war against **Iraq** opens. **U.S.** urges **Israel** to refrain from retaliating so as not to disrupt relations between **U.S.** and Arab countries in anti-**Iraq** coalition.

On Jan. 23, **Israel** announces it will not retaliate against missile attacks. Eventually **U.S.** Patriot missiles prove effective in countering Iraqi strikes.

On Jan. 30, **Israel** engages Palestinian guerrillas in southern **Lebanon** in response to Palestinian rocket attack. Action does not lead to opening of second front in war.

On Jan. 27, **Egypt** says aim of war should be elimination of **Saddam Hussein** as **Iraq**'s ruler.

On Jan. 26, Iraqi warplanes begin fleeing to Iranian airfields for safety.

On Jan. 29, **Iran** impounds Iraqi planes and refuses to return them even after war ends.

On Jan. 3, Voice of Free Iraq radio broadcasts from **Saudi Arabia** call upon Iraqis to overthrow **Saddam Hussein**.

On Jan. 14, military levels in **Saudi Arabia** reported to be 415,000 American and 265,000 coalition troops, as opposed to 545,000 Iraqi troops in **Kuwait**.

On Jan. 17, **Saudi Arabia** hit by Iraqi Scud missile as air war commences.

On Jan. 25, oil slick appears in **Persian Gulf**. **U.S.** accuses **Iraq** of deliberately causing it. Beginning of environmental castastrophe.

On Jan. 31, Arab troops supported by **U.S.** forces beat back Iraqi ground attack on Saudi city of Khafji.

On Jan. 9, meeting between Iraqi Foreign Minister Tariq Aziz and **U.S.** Secretary of State James Baker in Geneva fails to achieve breakthrough.

On Jan. 12, **U.S.** Congress votes authorization of use of force against **Iraq**. Vote in Senate is 52-47, in House of Representatives 250-183. Opponents of war resolution argue that economic sanctions should be given more time to work.

On Jan. 13, last minute trip to Baghdad by **U.N.** Secretary General Perez de Cuellar proves fruitless as **Saddam Hussein** stands firm.

Jan. 15, President **Bush** signs battle order. British parliament votes war authorization.

On Jan. 17, air war opens at 3 AM (in **U.S.**, 7 PM EST of Jan. 16). **Turkey** authorizes **U.S.** use of Incirlik airbase.

On Jan. 28, President **Bush** says that, after the war, **U.S.** will take the lead in solving Middle East problems.

◄ *The first ground battle of the war occurred on January 31 when Iraqi troops attacked the Saudi border town of Khafji. Allied troops quickly repelled the attackers.*

Feb. 1991

On Feb. 3, some 300,000 people rally in support of **Iraq** in Rabat, **Morocco**, despite **Morocco**'s role in the anti-**Saddam** coalition. Popular support for **Iraq** also reported in other Arab countries.

On Feb. 3, Syrian troops repel Iraqi exploratory attack across border into **Saudi Arabia**.

On Feb. 13, **Syria** affirms recognition of **Israel**'s right to exist in new Middle East political order anticipated with end of war.

On Feb. 6, **King Hussein**, facing enormous popular support for **Iraq** among Jordanians and Palestinians, abandons his neutrality and says impending war is "against all Arabs and all Muslims and not just **Iraq** alone."

On Feb. 12, **Saddam Hussein** confers with Soviet envoy about terms for Iraqi withdrawal from **Kuwait**.

On Feb. 15, Revolutionary Command Council indicates willingness to negotiate withdrawal. People of Baghdad celebrate possible end of war.

On Feb. 25, facing defeat under onslaught of invading coalition, Baghdad orders its army to withdraw from **Kuwait**.

On Feb. 28, **Iraq** orders its troops to stop fighting but does not acknowledge defeat.

◀ *Iraqi troops deserted by the thousands during the war. Many carried surrender notices dropped by allied aircraft over Iraqi positions.*

◀ *With allied victory assured, Iraqis in Kuwait City began a mass exodus back to Iraq in any vehicle they could find. Allied aircraft bombed the fleeing vehicles, turning the roadway into a "highway of death."*

March 1991

On March 10, **Syria** endorses **U.S.** Secretary of State Baker's idea of holding an Arab-Israeli peace conference under international auspices.

On March 12, Palestinian spokesman on **West Bank**, reflecting views of **PLO**, states that Palestinians desire the establishment of separate Palestinian state on the **West Bank** and **Gaza Strip** that would coexist with **Israel**. Discredited by its support for **Saddam Hussein**, the **PLO** is increasingly ignored in discussions of Arab-Israeli settlement; **West Bank** Palestinians become primary spokesmen.

On March 3, army accepts stringent coalition terms for ending war. Civil disorder begins in **Iraq** as Iraqi people, stimulated by **U.S.** propaganda calling for **Saddam Hussein**'s overthrow, take to the streets. Shiites in south seek to dominate major city of Basra. In north, **Kurds** take city of Sulaimaniya.

On March 5, the Revolutionary Command Council voids annexation of **Kuwait**.

The departing Iraqis set many Kuwaiti oil wells afire, causing major environmental problems. Shortly after the war ended, Iraq released its allied prisoners-of-war, including American flight surgeon Major Rhonda Cornum (right).

On Feb. 21, **Saudi Arabia** becomes center of activity for Iraqi opposition groups in exile.

On Feb. 24, ground war begins with attacks into **Kuwait** across Iraqi lines; sweeping "left hook" maneuver ultimately cuts off Iraqi retreat and traps most Iraqi units in **Kuwait** and southern **Iraq**.

On Feb. 26, Kuwait City retaken. From exile, Emir orders martial law. Kuwaiti underground assists in expulsion of Iraqis. Twenty-one of 43 Iraqi divisions reported out of action.

On Feb. 27, President **Bush** orders ground operations halted, thus ending fighting.

On Feb. 6, **U.S.** Secretary of State Baker says that new effort to resolve Arab-Israeli problem will be made after war.

On Feb. 12, **U.S.S.R.** envoy Primakov meets **Saddam Hussein** in **Iraq** to urge Iraqi withdrawal.

On Feb. 14, Soviet President Gorbachev requests postponement of ground war while new possibilities raised by Primakov mission are explored.

On Feb. 18, in Moscow, President Gorbachev gives Iraqi Foreign Minister Aziz a new formula for withdrawal.

On Feb. 19, fearful of the war ending with the Iraqi war machine still largely intact, President **Bush** announces that new Soviet plan is inadequate.

On Feb. 22, President **Bush** issues ultimatum for **Iraq** to withdraw from **Kuwait** by noon on Jan. 23. Iraqis begin setting fire to Kuwaiti oil wells. Eventually over 700 wells are set afire, causing severe environmental pollution.

On Feb. 24, ground war begins.

On Feb. 27, President **Bush** orders halt to ground offensive. Letter to **U.N.** announces Iraqi willingness to comply with all **U.N.** resolutions.

On March 11, **U.S.** Secretary of State Baker urges **Israel** to respond positively to "new thinking" on part of Arab states. Over following months **Yitzhak Shamir** shows great reluctance to commit **Israel** to peace conference with Arabs. Momentum for such a conference grows nevertheless.

On March 10, **Egypt** endorses **U.S.** Secretary of State Baker's postwar plan for an Arab-Israeli peace conference.

On March 30, in first meeting after the war, **Arab League** rejects all Iraqi efforts to justify occupation of **Kuwait**.

On March 8, **Iran** acknowledges encouraging Shiite rebellion in **Iraq**.

On March 27, President **Hashemi Rafsanjani** denies charges that Iranian troops and arms are helping rebels. He reaffirms that the **U.S.** is "still an enemy of the Islamic Revolution."

On March 4, Crown Prince Saad returns to **Kuwait**. Friction growing between Kuwaitis who stayed and those who fled.

On March 10, **Gulf Cooperation Council** endorses **U.S.** Secretary of State Baker's proposal for a general conference to resolve Arab-Israeli dispute.

On March 14, **Kuwait**'s ruler, **Jaber al-Sabah**, returns from exile.

On March 26, **U.N. Security Council** drafts plan to destroy all Iraqi nuclear, chemical, and biological weapons and orders **Iraq** to accept **Kuwait**'s borders as established in 1963.

Bush indicates willingness to see Shiite and Kurdish rebellion fail rather than risk dismemberment of **Iraq**.

43

(continued)

March 1991

Hafiz al-Asad of Syria ▶ (left) and Egypt's Husni Mubarak at the meeting in which they announced their opposition to the dismemberment of Iraq.

On March 16, **Saddam Hussein** promises democratic reforms in effort to quell popular uprising.

On March 20, **Saddam Hussein** appears on TV with 91-year-old Shiite leader Ayatollah Kho'i in appeal to Shiites to stop fighting. Despite his secular outlook, **Saddam** is willing to use religious appeals when expedient.

On March 28, Iraqi military and security forces gaining headway against rebel Shiites and **Kurds**.

April 1991

On Apr. 1, **Hafiz al-Asad** meets with **Husni Mubarak** in Cairo; they announce their opposition to dismemberment of **Iraq**.

On Apr. 2, Iraqi army crushes rebellion. **Kurds** begin to flee to Iranian and Turkish borders.

On Apr. 8, **U.S.** troops begin to withdraw from areas they occupy in southern **Iraq**.

On Apr. 12, **U.S.** forces undertake major relief effort for **Kurds** along Turkish border. Safe havens are secured in north by expelling Iraqi military.

On April 24, **U.S.** forces complete withdrawal from southern **Iraq**, turning over cease-fire observation duties to **U.N.**

The desperate situation of the ▶ Kurds after their failed rebellion led the U.S. to set up a major relief effort in areas along the Turkish border.

On March 20, **Kuwait** government resigns as disorder reigns and demands for greater political participation grow. Palestinians and other non-citizen Kuwaiti residents increasingly subjected to deportation and charges of collusion with Iraqis.

On March 22, rally for democracy in **Kuwait**.

On March 30, **Gulf Cooperation Council** cuts financial aid to **PLO** and **Jordan** as punishment for supporting **Saddam Hussein**.

On Apr. 1, **Mubarak** and **Syria**'s **Hafiz al-Asad** meet in Cairo and announce opposition to any splintering of **Iraq**, an often repeated fear during post-war Iraqi rebellion.

On Apr. 3, **Iran** welcomes Kurdish refugees from failed rebellion, asks for refugee aid from **U.N.** and foreign countries.

On Apr. 7, its facilities taxed to the limit, **Iran** stops taking in refugees after 500,000 have crossed border.

On Apr.1, as it becomes apparent that **Saddam Hussein** has survived crisis with his government intact, Saudi Minister of Information orders Saudi newspapers to quit criticizing him and to limit reporting on Iraqi rebellion.

On Apr. 7, Emir of **Kuwait** says that, "God willing," parliamentary elections may be held in 1992. Democracy advocates remain dissatisfied.

On Apr. 3, fearing exacerbation of long-standing Kurdish troubles within its own borders, **Turkey** blocks masses of Kurdish refugees from crossing frontier.

On Apr. 5, responding late and reluctantly to refugee tragedy, **U.S.** begins airdrops of supplies to **Kurds** along Turkish border.

On Apr. 8, **U.S.** troop withdrawal from **Iraq** begins.

On Apr. 11, **U.S.** and European countries agree to create safe havens for **Kurds** in northern **Iraq** so they can return to their homes.

On Apr. 12, **U.S.** army takes over Kurdish relief effort in northern **Iraq**. Refugees number 550,000 along both sides of Turkish border. Another 500,000-700,000 are on both sides of **Iraq**'s border with **Iran**.

On Apr. 20, autonomy talks begin between **Saddam Hussein** and Kurdish leaders.

On Apr. 24, last **U.S.** troops leave **Iraq**, leaving **U.N.** observers in their place.

◄ Kuwaitis returning to their country after the war found their houses damaged or destroyed and their stores burnt out and looted.

45

Central government increasingly in control of Beirut, but still under Syrian influence.

In Oct. and Nov., **Lebanon** participates in Madrid peace conference.

In Oct. and Nov., at Madrid peace conference, **Syria** shows inclination to compromise with **Israel** over the issue of the **Golan Heights.**

In late Oct., owing to **Israel**'s refusal to negotiate with known **PLO** members or Palestinians from the occupied territories, a new group of Palestinian leaders and spokesmen emerge. The group, indirectly guided by the **PLO**, meet with **Israel** in Madrid as part of the Jordanian delegation. The Jordanians and the Palestinians together show willingness to continue negotiations at a bilateral level with the aim of securing autonomy and eventually independence for Palestinians in the occupied territories.

U.N. inspection teams find increasing evidence of Iraqi nuclear weapons program as they carry out mandate to eliminate **Iraq**'s weapons of mass destruction.

Economic sanctions remain in place, causing great hardship for the Iraqi people.

Iraq refuses to export **oil** under the strict conditions set by the **U.N.**, arguing that such conditions jeopardize **Iraq**'s sovereignty.

◄ *American troops returning from the Persian Gulf were greeted with much celebration. The U.S. still retains an armed presence in the Middle East.*

From Aug. through Dec., the remaining western hostages held in **Lebanon** are released by their captors. The Americans include Edward Tracy (released Aug. 11), Jesse Turner (Oct. 22), Thomas Sutherland (Nov. 18), Joseph Cicippio (Dec. 2), Alann Steen (Dec. 3), and Terry Anderson (Dec. 4), the longest-held of the hostages. Also released on Nov. 18 was Church of England envoy Terry Waite.

By the end of 1991, all the U.S. hostages in Lebanon had been released. Below, former hostages (from left) Joseph Cicippio, Terry Anderson, and Alann Steen exalt in their freedom shortly after Anderson's release.
▼

Under strong **U.S.** pressure, **Israel** reluctantly agrees to participate in Madrid peace conference in late October. **Yitzhak Shamir**, the only head of state to head his country's delegation, shows little willingness to trade land for peace.

In Oct. and Nov., **Egypt** participates in the Madrid peace conference.

An Egyptian, Boutros Ghali, is elected to succeed Javier Perez de Cuellar as Secretary General of the **United Nations**. Ghali was part of **Anwar Sadat**'s delegation at the signing of the **Camp David Accords**.

Negotiations continue between the **U.S.** and the Arab states of the **Persian Gulf** regarding future security arrangements and possible basing rights and pre-positioning of the **U.S.** equipment.

In Oct.-Nov., Saudi delegation present in Madrid to observe the Arab-Israeli peace conference.

By Nov., most oil fires in **Kuwait** have been extinguished.

On Dec. 15, the last remaining **U.S.** combat troops leave **Kuwait**.

The **U.S.** persuades **Israel** and its Arab adversaries to attend a peace conference jointly sponsored by the **U.S.** and the **U.S.S.R. U.S.** Secretary of State Baker makes numerous trips to Middle East in pursuit of this goal.

On Oct. 18, the **U.S.S.R.** and **Israel** resume diplomatic relations as precursor to Arab-Israeli peace talks.

On Oct. 30, an Arab-Israeli peace conference opens in Madrid. After three days of plenary meetings, conference moves to stage two, and series of bilateral meetings between **Israel** and **Syria**, **Israel** and **Lebanon**, and **Israel** and **Jordan** dealing with such region-wide matters as arms control and water. After an initial stage two meeting, conference adjourns on Nov. 3 without firm agreement on where or when to meet again.

From Aug. through Dec., the remaining western hostages held in **Lebanon** are released by their captors.

Boutros Ghali of **Egypt** is elected to succeed Javier Perez de Cuellar as Secretary General of the **United Nations**.

In Dec., the **U.S.** withdraws its last remaining combat troops from **Kuwait**. **U.S.** troops will continue to train Kuwaiti soldiers.

On Dec. 10, another round of Arab-Israeli peace talks begins in Washington, D.C.

On Dec. 16, the **U.N. General Assembly** repeals 1975 resolution equating Zionism with racism.

On October 30, an Arab-Israeli peace conference gets underway in Madrid, Spain. Although nothing major is resolved, the conference, simply by bringing the opposing sides together, represents a major step toward peace in the Middle East.
▼

May-Dec. 1991

47

Civilians have suffered greatly in the turmoil that has beset the Middle East for decades. In Lebanon, the end of a 15-year civil war in 1990 gave the people a long-awaited opportunity to celebrate peace (above).

CRISIS IN THE MIDDLE EAST:

An Alphabetical Overview

ABDALLAH, KING (1882–1951). During World War I, T.E. Lawrence ("Lawrence of Arabia") helped persuade Sharif Hussein, the governor of Mecca, to declare himself in revolt against his overlord, the Ottoman Sultan, an ally with Germany and Austria-Hungary against Britain, France, and Russia. Sharif Hussein revolted in the name of Arab independence from Ottoman Turkish domination and sent two of his sons, Faisal and Abdallah, to lead the Arab tribal forces fighting in **Palestine** and **Syria** in the north. After the war, Britain ceased to favor immediate Arab independence, preferring to take control of **Iraq** and **Palestine** for itself (as League of Nation mandates), while France took over **Syria** and **Lebanon.** In 1920, the French chased Abdallah's brother Faisal

King Abdallah, the first king of Jordan, is the grandfather of the country's current ruler, King Hussein I.

out of **Syria,** where nationalists had proclaimed him king. The following year Britain secured his selection as king of **Iraq.** At the same time, in April 1921, the British offered Abdallah rule over the portion of its **Palestine** mandate territory east of the Jordan River. Abdallah ruled this country as Transjordan. When it achieved formal independence in 1946, he adopted the title of king and renamed his country the Hashemite Kingdom of **Jordan,** thus including a reference to his family's descent from the Prophet Muhammad's clan of Hashim. Abdallah secretly developed good working relations with the Zionists in the western part of **Palestine,** but nonetheless fought against **Israel** in 1948 to preserve Arab rule in the old city of **Jerusalem** and in major Arab towns to the north and south. In 1950, he incorporated this area, now generally known as the **West Bank,** into **Jordan,** and reaffirmed the name of his kingdom as applying to both sides of the Jordan River. In July 1951, he was assassinated as he entered the Al-Aqsa Mosque in **Jerusalem.**

ALGERIA, a country two-thirds the size of Alaska, stretches from the coast of the Mediterranean Sea due south of France to the southern fringes of the Sahara desert. Along some parts of the coast there are fertile plains and good seaports, such as Oran and Algiers, the capital. Though most of the country's 22 million people (mostly Arab but with a Berber minority) live in the north, which is also the country's industrial and agricultural center, Algeria's national income depends heavily on oil from deposits in the northern Sahara. Algeria was conquered by France in 1830 and turned into a colony. Heavy French settlement and close economic ties made the war of independence that

French president de Gaulle helped arrange the settlement through which Algeria gained independence from France.

began in 1954 costly for both sides. Under the leadership of the **National Liberation Front (FLN),** Algeria won the war and formally became independent on July 3, 1962. The **FLN** established a one-party state that ruled without significant challenge until 1990, when Muslim activists won most of the municipal elections. The election demonstrated not only a dissatisfaction with the **FLN**'s monopoly on power, but also discontent over failed socialist policies, economic stagnation, and unemployment.

ANGLO-IRANIAN OIL COMPANY. In 1908, **Iran** became the first Middle Eastern country to produce oil. The next year, the Anglo-Persian Oil Company was formed, which later changed its name to the Anglo-Iranian Oil Company (AIOC). A British firm with the British government as the major and controlling partner, the AIOC increasingly dominated the Iranian economy. Resentment over the small share of profits coming **Iran**'s way under the concession agreements sparked a call for nationalization of the oil industry after World War II. Prime Minister **Mohammed Mossadegh** touched off an international furor when he did just that in 1953. A successful international boycott of Iranian oil forced the reversal of the nationalization and contributed to **Mossadegh**'s fall from power. The AIOC was then transformed into the National Iranian Oil Company, and British ownership was reduced to 40 percent, with other foreign companies owning the rest. By 1973, however, **Iran** had assumed full control of the company.

ARAB LEAGUE. See the **League of Arab States.**

ARAB NATIONALISM began to evolve in the mid-19th century, when a number of Arab writers, mostly Christians, began to reassert the excellence of the Arabic literary language, which they felt had been in decline for centuries. Newfound pride in an Arab identity based on language was infused with political meaning early in the 20th century, when a few Arab intellectuals called for greater Arab autonomy within the increasingly

Gamal Nasser of Egypt was among the most prominent of the Arab nationalist leaders. His work on behalf of various Arab causes brought him great prestige in the Middle East.

Islam arose in the Arabian Peninsula. Mecca, Islam's holiest city, is in Saudi Arabia. All Muslims are required to make a pilgrimage to Mecca (above) once in their lives.

Turkish-oriented Ottoman Empire, or, in the case of **Egypt** and **North Africa,** freedom from European imperialism. After World War I, disagreements arose on matters of religion. Christian and Jewish Arabs saw Arab nationalism as separable from **Islam,** as did Arab nationalist leaders who feared an intrusion of religion into political affairs. While most nationalists visualized a single independent Arab state stretching from **Morocco** to **Iraq,** the reality of the new Arab states created, after World War I, from the wreckage of the Ottoman Empire and later, after World War II, during the process of decolonization, led some to put greater interest on local nationalisms, e.g., Syrian, or Egyptian, or Iraqi nationalism. **Gamal Abd al-Nasir (Nasser)** was the foremost Arab nationalist leader of the postwar period; he strove unsuccessfully to achieve Arab unity by creating the short-lived **United Arab Republic.** The **Ba'th Party,** which eventually came to power in both **Syria** and **Iraq,** is also dedicated to Arab nationalism, though the different branches of the party do not see eye to eye. Muslim political activism in the 1970s and 1980s was helped by a popular perception that even though the Arab nationalist movement had rid the Arab lands (excepting **Palestine**) of foreign domination, it had failed to provide better lives for the Arabs as a whole.

ARABIAN PENINSULA, a land mass two-thirds the size of Alaska, includes **Saudi Arabia, Kuwait, Bahrain, Qatar,** the **United Arab Emirates,** Oman, and **Yemen.** The peninsula is bordered by the Red Sea to the west, the Arabian Sea, and the Gulf of Oman to the south, the **Persian Gulf** to the east, and the Iraqi and Jordanian deserts to the north. Most of the region is desert, with an immense region of dunes in the south, the Empty Quarter, isolating the southern coast and its hinterland. **Yemen** and Oman, the countries along the southern coast, are comparatively fertile and have historic links with Africa and India. Most of the **Persian Gulf** coast is divided between the small states of the **United Arab Emirates, Qatar,** and **Kuwait,** with the island republic of **Bahrain** just off shore. The rest belongs to the Kingdom of **Saudi Arabia.** Oil, as well as sub-surface water, is found primarily along the Gulf coast, although commercially significant amounts also occur in Oman and **Yemen.** Traditionally, nomads traversed the vast wastes separating the well-populated and fertile south, the mountain oases of the west, and the fishing and trading towns of the **Persian Gulf.** Over the past 30 years, however, the entire region has experienced a profound economic transformation because of the influx of oil wealth.

ARAFAT, YASIR (1929–) is the leader of the **Palestine Liberation Organization (PLO).** Born in **Palestine** and educated as an engineer in **Egypt,** he

PLO leader Yasir Arafat addressed the United Nations General Assembly in 1974 (above).

led, in the 1950s, the Palestinian Students' Union and worked in **Kuwait** as an engineer. His guerrilla movement **al-Fatah** arose during this period, although the organization did not gain visibility until 1965. In 1968–69, after proving its military effectiveness fighting an Israeli raid against the town of Karameh in **Jordan, al-Fatah** became the leading constituent of the **PLO,** and Arafat became the **PLO** chairman. In that position, Arafat skillfully balanced the radical and moderate organizations within the **PLO,** built strong economic relations with **Kuwait** and **Saudi Arabia,** and successfully courted world opinion. Relations with **Jordan** and **Syria** proved more difficult, however. He reached a high point in 1974 when he addressed the **United Nations General Assembly.** The expulsion of the **PLO** from **Lebanon** after the Israeli invasion of 1982 and his support for **Saddam Hussein** in the Persian Gulf War of 1991 threatened his leadership. Skillful as always, Arafat reemerged as the paramount leader of the Palestinians and made important decisions leading to the Madrid Peace Conference in November 1991, even though he was not a participant.

ARAMCO (ARABIAN-AMERICAN OIL COMPANY) was organized in 1948 by Standard Oil of California, Texas Oil, Standard Oil of New Jersey (now known as Exxon), and Socony Vacuum as a consortium to explore for and produce oil in **Saudi Arabia.** Oil had first been discovered in 1938; subsequent exploration revealed that **Saudi Arabia** was sitting atop the largest reserve of oil in the world. Though relations with ARAMCO were generally good, in the 1960s **Saudi Arabia** began to create its own organizations for exploiting its petroleum wealth. **Saudi Arabia** began to take over ARAMCO in 1972 and became its sole owner in 1980. During this same period vast new oil revenues were transforming the kingdom.

Hafiz al-Asad has ruled Syria since 1970. In 1977, Asad (above left) conferred with U.S. president Jimmy Carter during a series of Middle East peace talks.

Though Americans and other foreign personnel remained important in ARAMCO operations, centered in the city of Dhahran, **Saudi Arabia**'s ultimate goal is to fully manage its own oil industry.

ASAD, HAFIZ AL-(1928–   ) assumed control of the presidency of **Syria** in a 1970 coup and has ruled dictatorially ever since. Hafiz al-Asad was educated at the Syrian military academy and rose to command the air force. He is a member of the minority Alawi sect of Shi'ite Muslims from northwest **Syria** and has favored the promotion of fellow Alawis to high government and military positions. While he has shown a willingness to use **terrorism** as a weapon, and has deployed his substantial military might in **Lebanon** and against Muslim political activists in his own country, he has been careful since his loss of the **Golan Heights** to **Israel** in the **Six-Day War** to avoid major conflicts with **Israel.**

BA'TH PARTY was founded in the mid-1930s by French-educated Syrians Michel Aflaq and Salah ad-Din Bitar and held its first party congress in 1947. The Ba'th ("Renaissance") Party is a secular, socialist party devoted to **Arab nationalism** and Arab unity. Since 1966, its regional branches controlling the governments of **Syria** and **Iraq** have been bitterly divided. **Hafiz al-Asad** and **Saddam Hussein,** the current rulers of **Syria** and **Iraq,** respectively, are also the leaders of the Ba'th party in those countries. Organizationally, the Ba'th resembles communism in its vision of itself as an elite guiding the masses and its demands for loyalty and obedience from rank-and-file members.

BAGHDAD PACT is the informal name of the series of economic and military agreements reached in 1955 between **Turkey,** Pakistan, **Iran,** Britain, and the **United States.** The Baghdad Pact represented an American vision of how to protect the Middle East from Soviet encroachment. Both

Although most of its oil deposits are exhausted, Bahrain, a tiny Persian Gulf emirate, has remained affluent by becoming one of the major financial centers of the Arabian Peninsula.

Iraq, as the only Arab member, and the pact itself were denounced by **Nasser**'s **Egypt** as an extension of the Cold War to the Middle East and a potential threat to **Egypt.** Such fears led to closer ties between **Egypt** and the **U.S.S.R.,** and the union of **Egypt** and **Syria** into the **United Arab Republic. Iraq** withdrew from the pact in 1958. The remaining regional members reformed themselves as the Central Treaty Organization (CENTO) and refocused their activities on economic and social matters. After the Iranian revolution of 1979, CENTO dissolved.

BAHRAIN, a **Persian Gulf** emirate, spreads over one large and 32 mostly uninhabited small islands in the gulf. Tiny Bahrain covers the same land area (260 square miles) as Memphis, Tennessee. Its population—over 400,000—is two-thirds native Arab Bahrainis (the majority of them Shi'ites) and one-third foreign workers. Bahrain became a British protectorate in the 19th century. The British withdrew in 1970 amid leftist and nationalist agitation that continued to disrupt the newly independent country until the emir suspended its national assembly in 1975. Since then, there have been numerous leftist and—after the Iranian Revolution —Shi'ite attempts to gain power. The ruling Khalifa family is Sunni Muslim. With plentiful fresh water, rich pearl fisheries, and an adventurous trading population, Bahrain was a major **Persian Gulf** center even before oil was discovered in 1932. Most of Bahrain's oil is now gone, but refining and industrial activities, focused particularly on a large aluminum smelting plant, give Bahrain a robust economy. It is also a major banking and telecommunications center. Since 1986, it has been linked to **Saudi Arabia** by a causeway.

BEGIN, MENAHEM (1913–   ), Israel's prime minister from 1977 to 1983, began his political career in the rightist, minority faction of Zionism known as the Revisionists. He succeeded Vladimir Jabotinsky as leader of the revisionists; but unlike Jabotinsky, he had a strongly religious view of Zionism. He founded the Irgun underground military organization to fight against Britain during the mandate period. Extreme acts of Irgun violence and extremist political views made Begin unpopular with the mainstream of Zionist leadership. Slowly, however, support for his Herut Party, later incorporated into the **Likud** bloc, grew until, in 1977, he achieved power. As prime minister, he boldly returned the Sinai peninsula, captured in 1967, to **Egypt** in return for peace. He nonetheless advocated extensive Jewish settlement and permanent Israeli control of the **West Bank.** The **Operation Peace in Galilee** invasion of **Lebanon** in 1982 discredited his government because it seemed to many Israelis to be a needless war that caused more suffering than it was worth. He retired and went into political seclusion in 1983.

BEN GURION, DAVID (1886–1973) was the political leader of the Jewish community (**Yishuv**) in **Palestine** from 1935 to 1948 and then **Israel**'s first prime minister until 1953. Ben Gurion was born in Poland, became a Zionist at age 17, settled in Palestine in 1906, and henceforth devoted all his energy to the growth of Zionism. He belonged to the majority labor faction of the Zionist movement, the precursor of the **Labor Party** and, in the 1920s, helped organize the Histadrut labor federation that subsequently became a cornerstone of **Israel**'s socialist economy. Although he left office in 1953, he ultimately returned for a second term as prime minister from 1955 to 1963, during which time he collaborated with Britain and France in the 1956 Suez War. He strongly opposed, both before and after **Israel**'s independence, the political policies of **Menahem Begin,** who became his most important successor as prime minister.

BOURGUIBA, HABIB (1903–) led **Tunisia** for 31 years. The French-educated Bourguiba, having grown impatient with the nationalist Destour Party then seeking independence for **Tunisia,** founded his own Neo-Destour Party in 1934. Several times imprisoned, he eventually negotiated independence from France in 1955–56. He was continuously re-elected president and ultimately proclaimed president for life in 1975. Modernist and pro-Western in inclination, he took a more moderate approach toward **Israel** than did leaders of other Arab countries. Despite this liberalism, the one-party rule of the Neo-Destour (after 1964 the Socialist Destour) eventually aroused political opposition, increasingly inspired by Islamic religious values and slogans. In 1987 he was forced into retirement because his increasing age had impaired his ability to rule.

After 31 years as ruler of Tunisia, Habib Bourguiba was forced from office and into retirement in 1987.

BUSH, GEORGE (1924–), U.S. president elected in 1988, was not particularly active in Middle Eastern affairs until the summer of 1990, when **Iraq** suddenly invaded **Kuwait.** Within days, Bush had committed the **United**

States irrevocably to the liberation of **Kuwait** and the restoration of its legitimate government. His skillful diplomacy and steadfast determination to overturn **Iraq**'s aggression led to the assembly of an unprecedented multinational military coalition and culminated in the Persian Gulf War in January and February of 1991. The coalition's spectacular success in defeating **Iraq** immensely increased the influence of the **United States** throughout the Middle East, although Bush was criticized for allowing **Saddam Hussein** to remain in power. Bush and his Secretary of State, James Baker, performed another great feat of diplomacy in persuading **Israel** and its Arab adversaries to sit down together at a peace conference in Madrid on October 30, 1991.

CAMP DAVID ACCORDS. In November, 1977, **Egypt**'s president, **Anwar Sadat,** startled the world by traveling to **Israel** (the visit had been secretly prepared by Egyptian and Israeli negotiators) and inaugurating a peace initiative. To facilitate negotiations, **U.S.** President **Jimmy Carter** invited **Sadat** and Israeli Prime Minister **Menahem Begin** to Camp David, the presidential retreat, to discuss peace. After several days of meetings the Camp David Accords were announced. They consisted primarily of two documents, one a general statement of principles to be followed in seeking a comprehensive settlement of the Arab-Israeli conflict, namely, an exchange of land for peace and a staged resolution of Palestinian demands for self-rule; the other, the outline for an Egyptian-Israeli peace treaty. The treaty was subsequently signed and went into effect on April 25, 1979. Negotiations on Palestinian self-rule broke down, however, and did not resume until the Madrid peace conference of 1991.

CARTER, JIMMY (1924–   ) was elected **U.S.** president in November 1976. A year later **Anwar Sadat** visited **Jerusalem** to begin a new peace initiative between **Israel** and **Egypt.** President Carter and his Secretary of State, Cyrus Vance, joined actively in the peace negotiations. After a meeting between **Menahem Begin** and **Sadat** at Camp David, the presidential retreat, the **Camp David Accords** were signed (September 1978), followed by an Israeli-Egyptian peace treaty six months later. Carter's personal diplomacy with the two heads of state was essential to the reaching of an agreement. Later in 1978, however, the **United States** was surprised by the rapid build-up of a revolutionary situation in **Iran,** a close **U.S.** ally. Cool relations with the provisional revolutionary government worsened when Carter decided in the fall of 1979 to admit the deposed Shah of Iran to the **United States** for medical treatment. In response, a radical revolutionary group seized the **U.S.** embassy in Teheran and took its personnel captive. The 444-day **hostage crisis** profoundly damaged Carter's reputation. Neither threats, nor negotiations, nor a military rescue attempt succeeded in securing the hostages' release before the day of **Ronald Reagan**'s inauguration as Carter's successor.

EGYPT is a country straddling the northeast corner of Africa and the adjoining Sinai peninsula in Asia. Although Egypt is one-third larger than Texas, it is so arid and so dependent on water from the Nile River that the arable area on which the bulk of the country's 55 million people live is less than twice the size of Massachusetts. Egypt adds 1 million people to its population every eight months; its capital, Cairo, has grown into

An Egyptian soldier (above) scans the Iraqi front during the 1991 Persian Gulf War. Egypt's contribution to the Allied coalition helped strengthen the country's ties to the U.S.

one of the largest cities in the world. Predominantly agricultural and with oil production barely sufficient for its own needs, Egypt is a very poor country deeply in debt. Yet as the largest Arab country, Egypt has long sought a leadership role in the Arab world. Though formally a part of the Ottoman Empire in the 19th century, Egypt was virtually independent and in control of its own economic and military affairs until 1882, when it was occupied by Britain. British domination remained, in one form or another, until 1952, when a military conspiracy known as the **Free Officers Movement** led a revolution that overthrew Egypt's king. Under the dynamic presidency of **Gamal Abd al-Nasir (Nasser)**, Egyptian leadership of the Arabs was generally acknowledged; but even with Soviet aid to build the mammoth Aswan High Dam, **Nasser**'s socialist policies could not make his country prosperous; nor was he able to defeat **Israel** in the **Six-Day War** of 1967. **Nasser**'s successor, **Anwar Sadat,** turned toward the **United States,** concluded a peace treaty with **Israel,** and opened up the country's economy with his *infitah* policy. These moves injured Egypt's standing in the Arab world. After **Sadat**'s assassination by Muslim fundamentalists angry at his peace with **Israel, Husni Mubarak** led Egypt back into favor with the other Arab states without weakening its close relations with the **United States.**

FAHD, KING (1921/22–   ), the ruler of **Saudi Arabia** since 1982 and the son of the kingdom's founder, King Abd al-Aziz, the latter also known as Ibn Saud. Among Abd al-Aziz's many sons, the full brothers of King Fahd form an influential group, including the current Minister of Defense, Prince Sultan. King Fahd came to power at a time of declining oil prices and thus has not benefited from the boom economy of his predecessor,

King Khalid. Early in his reign King Fahd expressed interest in a number of governmental reforms; none have thus far materialized, and he has generally followed a cautious and conservative course. King Fahd's acceptance of American leadership in the 1990 **Kuwait-Iraq** crisis and his willingness to host hundreds of thousands of coalition troops on Saudi territory signaled a new closeness in relations between the **United States** and **Saudi Arabia.**

FAISAL, KING (1904/5–75) ruled **Saudi Arabia** from 1964 to 1975. When **Saudi Arabia**'s founder, King Abd al-Aziz, died in 1953, his oldest son succeeded him as **King Saud.** He was in turn succeeded by Abd al-Aziz's second oldest son, Faisal, in 1964. The succession was not easy: **Saud** had been an irresponsible, wasteful monarch and was considered a poor ruler by many of his half-brothers; nonetheless, he had substantial support in the kingdom. A tug-of-war for control of the government began in 1958 and ended with **Saud**'s deposition. At the time, Prince Faisal was the principal figure appealing for more orderly and competent government. He began the process of modernizing the kingdom within an essentially conservative world view that emphasized the retention of basic religious values and institutions. This policy was continued by his two successors, King Khalid and **King Fahd.** He instituted comprehensive health and education programs, including education for women, but he did not live long enough to plan for the huge influx of oil wealth following the price rises of 1973–74. He was assassinated on March 25, 1975 by a nephew who felt he was avenging the death of his brother who had died in earlier riots protesting King Faisal's introduction of television to the kingdom. King Faisal is remembered throughout the Islamic world as an exceptionally pious, abstemious, and benevolent monarch.

FATAH, AL- is the Palestinian Arab guerrilla organization formed as a resistance movement by **Yasir Arafat** in the late 1950s; it officially commenced guerrilla activity in January 1965. The word *fatah* in Arabic means "victory"; the letters *h, t,* and *f* in the Arabic spelling of the name also form a reversed acronym for *Harakat Tahrir Filistin* or "Palestine Liberation Movement." The most effective of the many small Palestinian guerrilla organizations, al-Fatah became the dominant force on the National Council of the **Palestine Liberation Organization (PLO)** in 1968; the next year, **Arafat** became **PLO** chairman. In its armed struggle to free **Palestine,** al-Fatah engaged in terrorist attacks on civilian targets and guerrilla attacks on military ones. With ample financial support from **Saudi Arabia** and other Arab countries, and military support from the **U.S.S.R.,** it equipped and trained a force of some 10,000 fighting men. Al-Fatah and other guerrillas proved a significant obstacle to **Israel**'s plan to rout the **PLO** from **Lebanon** in 1982, although eventually the **PLO** forces were compelled to withdraw. Subsequently, al-Fatah changed its tactics, committing itself to seeking independence for only part of **Palestine** (the **West Bank** and **Gaza Strip**), formally recognizing **Israel**'s right to exist, and renouncing **terrorism.** By 1991, al-Fatah had lost much of its importance, largely through the assassination of its top leaders, presumably by **Israel;** its ill-conceived support for **Iraq** in the Persian Gulf War; a loss of financial support; and a shift of world attention to a fresh group of Palestinian leaders from within the occupied territories.

FLN (NATIONAL LIBERATION FRONT), the **Algeria** independence movement (in French, *Front de Liberation Nationale*), was founded secretly around 1954 by a group of young Algerian activists including Ahmed Ben Bella, who eventually became independent **Algeria**'s first president. Armed struggle against France began in 1954 and culminated, after a bitter war, in independence in 1962. The FLN then ruled **Algeria** as a socialist, one-party state until economic deterioration and popular discontent, highlighted by the 1989 bread riots in Algiers, forced the government to liberalize. In 1990, the growing power of Muslim political activists was demonstrated by FLN defeats in most municipal elections, although the FLN remained in control of the central government.

FREE OFFICERS MOVEMENT was the secret Egyptian military group that overthrew King Faruq on July 23, 1952. Formed in the 1940s of military officers drawn from the middle and lower classes, the Free Officers Movement was led by **Gamal Abd al-Nasir (Nasser)**, who formally became its chairman in 1950. General Muhammad Nagib, not a member of the movement, became the chairman of **Egypt**'s new ruling body, the Revolutionary Command Council. **Nasser** eased him from power and publicly took over as **Egypt**'s leader in 1954. **Anwar Sadat,** who succeeded **Nasser** after his death in 1970, was also one of the Free Officers.

GAZA STRIP is a small piece of land along the Mediterranean Sea at the juncture between Israeli and Egyptian territory. The strip has a land area somewhat larger than that of New York City and a population of over 600,000 Palestinian Arabs and a handful of Israeli settlers. Though the city of Gaza goes back to Biblical times and was the place where Samson met his death, the Gaza Strip had no separate identity until 1948. Before that it was simply part of **Palestine.** Refugees from the Arab-Israeli war of 1948 more than doubled the strip's population to 250,000. **Egypt** administered

Israeli occupation of the Gaza Strip has greatly agitated the area's Palestinian residents. Below, demonstrators confront Israeli soldiers during a protest march in December 1987.

the territory from 1948 until 1967, when it was captured by **Israel** in the **Six-Day War.** Its population has almost doubled during the years of Israeli occupation. Until the beginning of the *intifada* uprising against Israeli occupation in 1988, many Arabs from Gaza worked in **Israel.** Strikes and curfews have curtailed such employment, however, and the despondent mood of the population has fostered the rise there of Hamas, a religiously oriented Palestinian resistance movement. As a territory taken over in the 1967 war, the Gaza Strip is seen by the Arabs as a potential part of an independent Palestinian state. The **Likud** government of **Israel,** however, does not favor the return of the Gaza Strip to Arab rule.

GOLAN HEIGHTS was established as the border between **Syria** and **Israel** in 1948, following the precedent of an earlier agreement between Britain and France when they were ruling the two countries as mandatories. The agreement left **Syria** in control of high land overlooking Israeli settlements around the Sea of Galilee and in the upper **Jordan** valley. Syrian artillery frequently shelled these towns, and seizure of the Golan Heights was an important Israeli military objective in the **Six-Day War** of 1967. **Syria** ultimately lost a sparsely populated region of some 720 square miles. Further Israeli military advances in the 1973 war were followed by a **U.S.**-mediated and **U.N.**-enforced disengagement agreement by which **Syria** regained control of the city of Quneitra, the largest town in the region. In 1981, **Israel** extended Israeli law to the Golan Heights, a move seen as tantamount to annexation. At the Madrid peace conference in 1991, return of the Golan Heights was the paramount Syrian demand.

GULF COOPERATION COUNCIL (GCC). The outbreak of war between **Iran** and **Iraq** in 1980 cast a pall of fear over the weaker Arab states of the **Persian Gulf** region. In response, **Saudi Arabia, Kuwait,** the **United Arab Emirates, Qatar, Bahrain,** and Oman formed the Gulf Cooperation Council to foster closer economic, political, and military relations. The GCC has proven an effective organization for bringing these states together, but it is reluctant to consider admitting the more populous and powerful states of **Iran** and **Iraq** to its membership.

HASSAN II, KING (1929–   ), ruler of **Morocco,** succeeded his father King Muhammad V in 1961. The legitimacy of his monarchy rests on his descent from the Prophet Muhammad and his symbolic leadership of the Moroccan Muslim community. Hassan was educated in French as well as Arabic and studied law in Bordeaux, France. When **Morocco** gained independence from France in 1956, Hassan, then crown prince, became head of the armed forces and later deputy prime minister. He has weathered several attempted coups and assassinations and maintains tight reins on government officials. In 1975, when Spain withdrew from Spanish Sahara, which borders **Morocco** to the south, King Hassan claimed the land for **Morocco** and called for a "Green March" of Moroccan civilians to occupy it. Demands for independence by local Saharans, backed by **Algeria,** led to a prolonged guerrilla war between **Morocco** and the POLISARIO (People's Organization for the Liberation of Saguia al-Hamra and Rio del Oro). King Hassan has maintained a comparatively friendly attitude toward **Israel,** while at the same time supporting Palestinian demands for independence.

In November 1979, Iranian radicals seized the U.S. embassy in Teheran and held its diplomatic and military personnel hostage for 444 days. The prolonged crisis undermined the Carter administration.

HOSTAGE CRISIS. In October 1979, **U.S.** President **Jimmy Carter** admitted the deposed Shah of Iran to the **United States** for medical treatment. Ostensibly in response, though also to impart a more radical tone to the Iranian Revolution, militant Muslim students seized the **U.S.** embassy in Teheran on November 4 and took prisoner some 50 diplomats and military personnel. The moderate leader of the provisional government, Mehdi Bazargan, who with his Foreign Minister Ibrahim Yazdi had met with **Carter**'s national security adviser Zbigniew Brzezinski in Algiers just two days earlier, was forced to resign along with his cabinet. The Islamic Revolutionary Council took over **Iran**'s government and oversaw a constitutional referendum, presidential election, and national assembly election during the following months. In the meantime, the Americans were held hostage, and the **Carter** administration fell into ever deeper despair as the months passed. Neither economic pressure (in the form of freezing $10 billion in Iranian assets) nor a military rescue attempt on April 25, 1980, gained their release. The hostage crisis contributed to **Carter**'s defeat by **Ronald Reagan,** and the hostages were not released until the day of **Reagan**'s inauguration, 444 days after they were initially taken.

HUSSEIN, KING (1935–   ) ascended to the throne of **Jordan** in 1952, at the age of 17, succeeding his father Talal, who had been removed from power because of mental problems. His prior education had been at Victoria College, an elite British-style preparatory school in Alexandria, **Egypt,** and at Sandhurst Military Academy in Britain. His rule of 40 years has been marked by assassination and coup attempts, war with **Israel** in 1967, a struggle against the **PLO** for control of **Jordan** in 1970, and severe economic problems brought on by his qualified support of **Saddam Hus-**

sein in the Persian Gulf War of 1991. Until the recent crisis, caused partly by a cessation of financial support from **Saudi Arabia** and partly by the return to **Jordan** of **Palestinians** expelled from **Kuwait, Jordan** had experienced steadily growing prosperity under his rule. He has been a generally popular ruler despite his reluctance, until recently, to open his government to democratic influences. His relations with Britain, the **United States, Israel, Syria,** and the **Palestinians** have been highly complicated and sometimes overly cautious. His current wife, the former Lisa Halabi, is the daughter of an American of Arab background. She converted to **Islam** and was given the name Nur al-Hussein (Noor).

HUSSEIN, SADDAM (1937–), the president of **Iraq,** was born in the town of Takrit to a poor family. In 1959, he went into exile in **Egypt** after taking part in an unsuccessful attempt to assassinate President Abd al-Karim Qasim. There he studied law and continued to work in politics. In 1963, after Qasim's overthrow, he returned to **Iraq** and became part of the **Ba'th Party** leadership structure. A skillful and ruthless political infighter, he rose rapidly, becoming the de facto head of government in 1969, one year after the **Ba'th Party** seized power in a coup. In 1979, he finally attained the presidency after the retirement of Ahmad Hasan al-Bakr. His ruthlessness and dictatorial methods combined with a cult of personality to make him the most powerful and visible ruler in the Arab world. He suppressed all internal opposition and went to war with **Iran** in 1980 to forestall Islamic political agitation. The war ended in 1988 with **Iraq** holding the upper hand, but deeply in debt and without the resources necessary to rebuild the country and reward the people for their sacrifices. Saddam ordered the invasion of **Kuwait** in 1990 to punish **Kuwait** for unfriendly behavior and to seize **Kuwait**'s wealth. Unable to back down without losing face, Saddam took his country into war against the **U.S.**-led coalition in 1991 and suffered a momentous defeat. Nevertheless, he remained in power, with **U.S.** acquiescence, and suppressed internal revolts by Shi'ites and **Kurds.** An intelligent, willful ruler with a sense of destiny and ruthless determination, Saddam Hussein remains a major force in Middle Eastern politics.

Iraqi president Saddam Hussein managed to hold onto power despite his stunning defeat in the Persian Gulf War.

INFITAH, the Arabic word for "opening," is used to describe **Anwar Sadat**'s 1974 decision to open **Egypt**'s socialist economy to foreign investment. This new initiative resulted in increased foreign investment in banking and the oil sector. Although some Egyptian businessmen reaped substantial benefits, the Egyptian economy in general remained stagnant.

In the late 1970s, Teheran was shaken by massive demonstrations against the shah. The revolution eventually led to the formation of a government based on Islamic principles.

INTIFADA is the Palestinian uprising against Israeli occupation of the **West Bank** and **Gaza Strip** that began in December 1987. Rather than guns and bombs, the main weapons of the *intifada* have been strikes, boycotts, graffiti, and thrown stones; many of the participants have been children. **Israel**'s efforts to subdue the uprising initially included the deliberate breaking of demonstrators' bones and other tactics that deeply offended world opinion. Loss of life on the Palestinian side approached 1,000 after four years, including Arabs killed by other Arabs on suspicion of collaboration with **Israel;** fewer than 100 Israelis have died. The uprising has closed schools, increased unemployment, and generally devastated the economy of the **West Bank** and **Gaza Strip;** it has also dispelled the illusion that the Arabs of the occupied territories do not object too strenuously to Israeli rule. The *intifada* also prompted the emergence of new spokesmen among the **Palestinians,** as well as the growth of a new, militant resistance movement, Hamas, ideologically based on **Islam.**

IRAN, a Texas-sized country of mostly deserts and mountains, is bordered by the Caspian Sea and the Soviet Union to the north, the **Persian Gulf** and Indian Ocean to the south, Afghanistan and Pakistan to the east, and **Iraq** and **Turkey** to the west; Teheran is its capital. Iran has historically been a strategic political and cultural crossroads. Its population of over 50 million is mostly Persian, but there are large minorities of Arabs in the southwest and Turks in the northwest. Iran remained a nominally independent kingdom during the years of imperialist encroachment on the Middle East in the 19th and early 20th centuries, although British and

Russian influence was so pervasive that many Iranians thought their rulers were selling the country out to foreign powers. Nationalist sentiments helped spark a constitutional revolution in 1906, but the government frustrated the working of the constitution until 1925, when the monarchy was overthrown by an army leader, Reza Khan, who crowned himself Reza Shah Pahlavi the next year. Reza Shah was deposed by Great Britain in 1941, and his son **Mohammed Reza Pahlavi** became ruler of a country under British and Soviet military occupation. When World War II ended, the young Shah proved an ineffective ruler. His prime minister, **Mohammed Mossadegh,** captured the country's nationalist sentiment by nationalizing the **Anglo-Iranian Oil Company** in 1951. Faced with **Mossadegh**'s growing popularity, the Shah fled the country in 1953, only to be restored by a coup engineered by American and British intelligence. The Shah henceforth ruled with a stronger hand and relied heavily on American advice and support. He also benefited from changes in oil policies that brought Iran much more money. After 1974, Iran modernized very rapidly, but opposition to the Shah grew just as rapidly. In 1979, he was overthrown in an almost bloodless Islamic Revolution led by the stern patriarchal figure of **Ayatollah Khomeini.** Thus a new country was born, the Islamic Republic of Iran. The Islamic Republic has endured an eight-year war with **Iraq,** as well as virtual ostracism from the world community because of its rigid religious policies and efforts to spread Islamic revolution abroad. Iran faces difficult economic problems and a rapidly growing population, but its size and ideological stance still make it an important factor in Middle East politics.

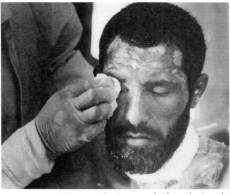

The use of poison gas by Iraq during the Iran-Iraq War violated international treaties banning such weapons.

IRAN-IRAQ WAR began on September 22, 1980, when **Iraq** invaded **Iran** on the pretext that **Iran** had failed to abide by all provisions of the 1975 Algiers agreement settling border issues between the two countries. **Iraq**'s actual objective was to overthrow the newly formed Islamic Republic of **Iran,** which had been fomenting unrest in **Iraq,** or at least to blunt **Iran**'s capacity for military expansion. The war lasted until 1988 with casualties approaching 1 million killed and wounded on both sides. The use of poison gas by **Iraq** and of human wave tactics by **Iran** gave it a particularly grim and cruel cast. Once the initial Iraqi advances had been reversed and **Iraq** went on the defensive in 1985, concern began to grow that **Iraq** might lose the war. This fear led the **United States** to tilt decisively toward **Iraq** and to build up its naval power in the **Persian Gulf** in an effort to intimidate **Iran**—despite **Iraq**'s apparently accidental attack on the *U.S.S. Stark,* in which 37 American sailors were killed. With **Iraq** achieving fresh gains on the battlefield and **Iran** having a difficult time supplying its army because of an international embargo on arms shipments, **Iran** finally accepted a **U.N.** ceasefire resolution in August 1988. **Ayatollah Khomeini** likened this agreement to end the war with **Saddam Hussein** still in power to "taking poison."

IRAQ was created after World War I out of three former provinces of the Ottoman Empire: Mosul, Baghdad, and Basra. It occupies nearly 168,000 square miles (a bit bigger than California) of what used to be called Mesopotamia, the valley of the Tigris and Euphrates rivers, an area rich with archaeological interest. The northern province of Mosul is home to Iraq's large Kurdish population (Sunni Muslims) and also contains valuable oil fields around Kirkuk. Baghdad, the capital, and the province around it are mostly Arab with a mixed Sunni and Shi'ite population. Basra, at the head of the **Persian Gulf,** is Arab and heavily Shi'ite. Overall, Shi'ites somewhat outnumber Sunnis, and the Arab Sunnis that dominate the current Ba'thist government are distinctly in a minority in the country at large. Britain received a mandate over the new state from the League of Nations and installed a monarchy there headed by its Arabian wartime ally Faisal, who had been expelled from his short-lived kingdom in **Syria.** Iraq became formally independent in 1932, but Britain continued to dominate it until a revolution in 1958 overthrew the monarchy. The Communist Party and the **Ba'th Party** competed for popularity under the frequently changing revolutionary regimes until 1963, when the Ba'thists finally achieved lasting supremacy. Though Iraq's population is only about 18 million, its leaders have sought supremacy in the Arab world. Oil wealth and friendship with the **U.S.S.R.** enabled Iraq to build a formidable army, but a prolonged stalemate in the **Iran-Iraq War** followed by defeat in the Persian Gulf War left the country seriously damaged and its army greatly weakened. Yet the dictatorship of **Saddam Hussein** continues.

ISLAM is the religion of the great majority of the people living in the Middle East. Based upon divine revelations made to the Prophet Muhammad between A.D. 610 and his death in A.D. 632, which were later collected into a book known as the Quran (or Koran), Islam views itself as a purification of the earlier religions of Christianity and Judaism. Islam means "submission" to the will of God. An individual believer is called a Muslim, or "submitter." Though Arab Muslims conquered an enormous empire in the Middle East and **North Africa** between the Prophet's death and 750, conversion of the conquered populations was a gradual, voluntary process that took three or four centuries. Substantial Christian minorities survive to this day in **Egypt, Syria,** and **Lebanon.** Islam stresses the oneness of God, the prophethood of Muhammad, and the brotherhood of all believers. Until the late 19th century, Islam framed the social, cultural, and political lives of most Middle Easterners. Secular nationalism challenged Islam for popular allegiance in the 20th century with great success. Then, in the 1960s, a gradual return to Islam began to gain headway (a phenomenon called **Muslim fundamentalism** in the West), achieving its first great success in the Iranian Revolution of 1979. Sunni Muslims originally differed from Shi'ite Muslims on the issue of leadership of the community, the former believing that the community should reach a consensus on matters and the latter feeling that leadership was divinely ordained for some descendant of Muhammad's cousin and son-in-law Ali, hence the full name *Shi'at Ali,* "Party of Ali." Today, Shi'ites constitute about 10 percent of the world Muslim community, but the great majority of the Iranian population and a smaller majority of the population in **Iraq, Lebanon,** and **Bahrain.**

Iraq's attempt to draw Israel into the Persian Gulf War failed, despite several Scud missile attacks on Tel Aviv and other Israeli cities.

ISRAEL came into being on May 14, 1948, after decades of turmoil and conflict between the native Arab population of **Palestine** and the community of Jewish settlers, the **Yishuv.** The war that followed its declaration of independence fixed Israel's borders to encompass 8,019 square miles, an area the size of New Jersey; no final constitutional determination of Israel's borders has ever been made. Israel is the final achievement of the Zionist movement that originated in the late 19th century to establish a homeland for the Jewish people. Britain, as the League of Nations mandatory for **Palestine,** tried to manage the conflicting claims and needs of **Palestine**'s Jewish and Arab populations, but eventually gave the task over to the **United Nations** in 1947. The **U.N.** voted to create two states, one Jewish and the other Arab, but the Arab state never came into being. Israel is an avowedly Jewish state, even though its 600,000 Arabs live as citizens alongside its 3.5 million Jews. Immigrating Jews are granted citizenship upon arrival; Arabs cannot immigrate. While most of the Jews in the **Yishuv** were immigrants from Europe, most Israeli Jews now trace their roots to **Morocco, Egypt, Iraq, Yemen, Syria,** and **Iran.** Ever mindful of the horror of the Holocaust, and having fought five wars against Arab opponents, Israel is deeply concerned with issues of military strength and security and extremely reluctant to hand the **West Bank, Gaza Strip, and Golan Heights,** territories seized in 1967, over to the Arabs. Some Israelis hope to retain these territories permanently, and thus enthusiastically support the building of Jewish settlements in them.

JERUSALEM is a sacred city to Christians, Jews, and Muslims alike. Located in the Judaean hills, it is officially the capital of **Israel** and, at the same time, is considered by the Palestinians to be their capital. The 1948 war left it a divided city with **Jordan** ruling the old city where the Dome of the Rock (Muslim), the Church of the Holy Sepulcher (Christian), and the Western or Wailing Wall (Jewish) are located, and **Israel** ruling west Jerusalem. A fortified line marked the division. The barriers were torn down in 1967 when **Israel** gained control of the entire city. The status of Jerusalem is considered the most difficult barrier to lasting peace between Arabs and Israelis.

JORDAN is a Arab country about the size of Maine that came into existence after World War I. It was during that postwar period that Britain granted its wartime ally, Emir **Abdallah** (later King), rule over the largely desert eastern portion of **Palestine,** which Britain controlled under a League of Nations mandate. The small town of Amman became the capital of the new state, then called Transjordan. In 1946, Transjordan became an independent country under the name Hashemite Kingdom of Jordan. In 1948–49, in the course of its war with the newly proclaimed state of **Israel,** Jordan captured the territory west of the Jordan River now called the **West Bank,** including the old city of **Jerusalem,** and annexed them. At that time Jordan also received 400,000 **Palestinian refugees,** and with a further refugee influx after the **Six-Day War** in 1967, Palestinians have come to number over half the Jordanian population of 3.5 million. Jordan lost the **West Bank** to **Israel** in 1967, and there has been subsequent disagreement between Jordanians and Palestinians as to whether that territory should ultimately—if **Israel** ever agrees—return to Jordan or become an independent Palestinian state. King **Abdallah**'s grandson King **Hussein** has ruled Jordan since 1952 and has been very cautious about introducing democratic institutions.

KHAMENEI, AYATOLLAH (1939–   ) was elected president of the Islamic Republic of **Iran** in 1981 and re-elected in 1985. Born in the city of Mashhad, Ali Khamenei studied religion with **Ayatollah Khomeini** and other prominent religious authorities. From 1964 on, he worked as a revolutionary activist, and was several times imprisoned during the Shah's reign. **Ayatollah Khomeini** expressed complete trust in him, and, when **Khomeini** died in 1989, Khamenei was chosen to succeed him as *vali faqih,* or "governing religious jurist." At that time, he began to be referred to as Ayatollah, a high rank in Shi'ite **Islam.**

KHOMEINI, AYATOLLAH RUHOLLAH (1902–1989), the leader of **Iran**'s Islamic revolution. He was trained as a cleric and showed an early interest in philosophy and mysticism. His first political actions came in 1944, when he spoke against the ruling **Pahlavi** family and called on fellow clerics to work to restore **Islam** in **Iran.** In the 1950s, he was a very successful teacher of Islamic law in the religious center of Qom. In the 1960s, he began leading public campaigns against the government. He was exiled after a major clash in 1963, but continued to attack the government from abroad. Holding the highest clerical rank, Ayatollah al-Uzma, he had many followers and was the natural person to turn to as leader of the 1979 revolution. His theory of "governance of a religious jurist" (*vilayet-i faqih*) was written into the constitution of the Islamic Republic of **Iran;** he held the post of *vali faqih* until his death. While not taking an active interest in day-to-day governmental affairs, his prestige in **Iran** was so immense that he truly dominated the country. Hundreds of thousands of distraught mourners attended his funeral in 1989.

KURDS are a linguistic and ethnic group numbering about 16.5 million people spread over parts of **Turkey, Iran, Iraq, Syria,** the **U.S.S.R.,** and **Lebanon.** The Kurdish language is related to Persian and completely unrelated to Arabic. Tribally organized Sunni Muslims, many Kurds still follow a traditional life-style based on farming and herding animals in mountain pastures. Kurdish political leaders have been seeking independence since World War I. They have repeatedly fought against the Turkish, Iraqi, and Iranian governments to achieve nationhood in the mountainous provinces of northwest **Iran,** northern **Iraq,** and southeastern **Turkey,** but they have never succeeded. Various other countries, including the **United States** and **Israel,** have sometimes encouraged their national aspirations for their own purposes with the result that the Kurds have been repeatedly victimized for generations.

KUWAIT is a wealthy Hawaii-sized emirate whose 2 million people (40 percent citizens, the rest foreign workers) live mostly in its capital city, also named Kuwait. The port of Kuwait was taken over by the Arab Utab tribe in the 18th century. Over the next 200 years, the British intermittently supported the sovereignty of the Emir of Kuwait; in 1914, Britain formally took Kuwait under its protection. Nevertheless, when **Iraq** gained independence after World War I, the new government claimed that Kuwait actually belonged to **Iraq,** a claim that **Iraq** has pressed from time to time up to the invasion of 1990. Kuwait became independent of Britain in 1961. Meanwhile, oil had been discovered in 1938, and oil exports began after World War II. Oil has made Kuwait one of the world's richest countries per capita and therefore a tempting target for neighboring **Iraq** and **Iran.** A parliament has twice been established and then suspended; the ruling **Sabah** family shows little interest in sharing power. In the aftermath of the Persian Gulf War in 1991, the power of the **Sabah** family was reestablished, and hundreds of thousands of Palestinians, many of whom had always lived in Kuwait, were expelled.

LABOR PARTY was the dominant political party in **Israel** until 1977, when a **Likud** government came to power. Socialist in ideology and strongly supported by Jews of European ancestry, it represents the continuation of the main current of the the Zionist movement from pre-independence times. Prime ministers from Labor include **David Ben Gurion** (1948–53, 1955–63), Moshe Sharett (1954-55), Levi Eshkol (1963–69), Golda Meir (1969–74), Yitzhak Rabin (1974–77), and Shimon Peres (1984–86).

LEAGUE OF ARAB STATES, or **Arab League,** as it is usually known, was founded with British encouragement on March 22, 1945, originally with only seven members. As more states became independent, however, its membership grew to 21, including the **PLO** as a full member. The headquarters of the League were transferred from Cairo to Tunis in 1979 after **Egypt** was expelled for violating Arab solidarity and making peace with **Israel.** In 1988, **Egypt** was readmitted, and the headquarters returned to Cairo. The **Arab League** has been more effective in cultural than in political matters, and the organization has not lived up to early hopes that it might be a step toward Arab unity. A majority of League members voted against **Iraq** in the Persian Gulf War crisis, but a substantial minority either voted with **Iraq** or abstained.

LEBANON, a country smaller than Connecticut, is inhabited by a complex mixture of religious groups. Though no census has been taken since 1936, it is now believed that Shi'ite Muslims form the largest community, mostly in the south and interior Biqa' valley. The second largest group, Maronite Christians, live mostly in Beirut and the mountains to the north. Next come Sunni Muslims, who are concentrated mostly in Beirut and the city of Tripoli. Last come Greek Orthodox and Druze (a religious offshoot from **Islam**). Starting in Ottoman times and continuing under French mandate after World War I, communal balance has been an important factor in Lebanese government. The French enlarged Lebanon, adding southern and interior regions, to make the country economically viable, although this step complicated the communal problems. Lebanon prospered enormously after independence in 1943, and Beirut grew into the banking and intellectual center of the Middle East—a showcase of free enterprise in a region largely dominated by socialism. Communal problems, particularly the exclusion of the Shi'ites from real power, were compounded by the **PLO**'s decision to base its operations in Lebanon after being expelled from **Jordan** in 1970. Civil war broke out in 1975 and continued until 1990, when Syrian power and influence finally brought it under control. **Syria** now dominates most of Lebanon while **Israel** controls a ''security zone'' in the south through a proxy South Lebanon Army.

LIBYA is a largely desert Texas-sized country in northeast Africa bordered by **Egypt, Tunisia,** and **Algeria.** Liberated in World War II from four decades of Italian rule, it became an independent kingdom in 1952. At first desperately poor, Libya suddenly found itself rich when it began exporting oil in 1961. In 1969, King Idris, originally a religious and tribal leader, was overthrown by Captain **Mu'ammar Qadhdhafi,** a young admirer of **Egypt**'s **Gamal Abd al-Nasir (Nasser).** After **Nasser**'s death in 1970, **Qadhdhafi** became a leading advocate of Arab unity and supporter of the Palestinian cause. His ideology has had little impact outside Libya, how-

A civilian carries his wounded child to safety among the debris of war-torn Beirut. The capital city bore the brunt of the 15-year-long civil war in Lebanon.

ever. Though Libya, personified by its dictatorial ruler **Qadhdhafi,** has become best known for meddling in other countries' affairs and supporting **terrorism,** a $25 billion project to pipe subsurface water from the Sahara desert to northern Libya for irrigation seems likely to change the country dramatically.

LIKUD is a right-wing Israeli political bloc based on the Herut party of **Menahem Begin. Begin** succeeded Vladimir Jabotinsky as leader of the Revisionist wing of the Zionist movement but was castigated as a right-wing demagogue by **Labor Party** leaders in the early days of independence. Likud came to power in 1977 and has been the dominant political force in **Israel** ever since. It derives much of its support from Jews of non-European ancestry.

MOROCCO is a California-sized Arab country located at the juncture of the Atlantic Ocean and Mediterranean Sea at the northwest corner of Africa. It encompasses a broad coastal plain, the high mountains of the Atlas range, and the fringes of the Sahara desert. Approximately 45 percent of its 25 million citizens speak one of three Berber languages unrelated to Arabic, but Arabic is the official language, and Morocco is therefore considered an Arab country. Morocco was a French protectorate from 1912 to 1956 when Sultan Muhammad V, who had previously been exiled in the midst of nationalist violence, became king of an independent Morocco. He was succeeded by his son **Hassan II** in 1961. The early days of the kingdom were marked by a struggle between the throne and the nationalist groups that had struggled for independence, but King **Hassan II** has become a dominating monarch.

MOSSADEGH, MOHAMMED (1880–1967) was the Nationalist prime minister of **Iran** from 1951 to 1953. A government official and member of the aristocracy under the Qajar dynasty, Mossadegh protested the rise to power of the **Pahlavi** dynasty in 1925. He returned to government as a national assembly (Majles) member in 1944 and became prominent as an opponent of Russian encroachment in northern **Iran** and of the **Anglo-Iranian Oil Company (AIOC).** He became prime minister after the Majles supported nationalization of the **AIOC** in 1951. As his power and popularity grew, a political crisis developed during which Shah **Mohammad Reza Pahlavi** fled the country in 1953; the Shah was soon restored when a coup supported by **U.S.** and British intelligence agents overthrew Mossadegh. Mossadegh spent the rest of his life under house arrest.

MUBARAK, HUSNI (1928–   ), the current president of **Egypt,** commanded the Egyptian air force during the **October War** of 1973 and, in 1975, was made vice president by **Anwar Sadat** in recognition of his effective leadership. He supported **Sadat** in the peace initiative toward **Israel** and, in 1981, took over as **Egypt**'s president after **Sadat** was assassinated. As president, he has been a systematic, hard-working administrator with little ability to stimulate popular excitement. He has followed the policies of **Sadat** and has succeeded in reestablishing **Egypt**'s good standing with the rest of the Arab world, a relationship damaged by the Egyptian-Israeli peace treaty. Although he has maintained a firm relationship with the **U.S.,** relations with **Israel** have become cooler during his presidency.

MUSLIM BROTHERHOOD, or *Ikhwan al-Muslimun,* was founded in 1929 as a religious, social, and political organization emphasizing self-help and strict Muslim values. The Brotherhood played a major role in Egyptian politics before and after World War II, wielding influence through demonstrations and assassination as well as elections. It strongly supported the war against **Israel** in 1948. Brotherhood power waned by 1949, and the organization was suppressed in 1954 after an assassination attempt against **Gamal Abd al-Nasir (Nasser).** The subsequent revival of the Muslim Brotherhood, guided by the revolutionary ideological writings of Sayyid Qutb, has made it the most important organization in the current movement of Muslim politics (**Muslim fundamentalism**). Muslim Brotherhood organizations exist in many Arab countries, and they have close relations with other Muslim organizations. In 1982, the Syrian army killed thousands of Brotherhood members in an assault on the city of Hama.

MUSLIM FUNDAMENTALISM is a term widely used in the **United States** to describe a broad range of Muslim political activist groups and activities

Muslim fundamentalism has swept through many Middle East countries. Ayatollah Khomeini, who led Iran's Islamic government for 10 years, was a prominent leader of the movement.

that became publicly visible to the West in the 1970s. The term is something of a misnomer, however, in that it suggests a religious attitude akin to that of Christian fundamentalists. In actuality, the Muslim groups differ substantially both from Christian fundamentalists and from one another. Some groups seek to gain influence through elections, publications, and winning popular favor by means of effective social programs. Others are violently revolutionary. Still others focus on moral rather than political matters. Religiously, some groups have conservative outlooks while others feature leftist or other innovative interpretations of **Islam**. Basing themselves on religious thinkers such as **Iran**'s **Ayatollah Khomeini, Egypt**'s Sayyid Qutb, and **Iraq**'s Muhammad Bakr Sadr, Muslim political activists have become extremely popular, particularly among students, small shopkeepers, and poor families new to the big cities.

NASIR, GAMAL ABD AL-(NASSER) (1918–1970), the most important figure in modern Arab politics, is usually referred to in English simply as Nasser. He fought well in **Egypt**'s war against **Israel** in 1948–49, rising to the rank of colonel. He came to political prominence in 1952 when he led the **Free Officers Movement** in a coup that overthrew **Egypt**'s King Faruq. After the coup, the Revolutionary Command Council was headed by General Muhammad Nagib until 1954, when Nasser took control personally. He rapidly became the paramount leader in the Arab world with enthusiastic popular followings in every country. Numerous political parties arose espousing "Nasserism," a personalized form of **Arab nationalism.** His popularity and world influence peaked after the failure of Britain, France, and **Israel** to defeat him in the Suez crisis and war of 1956. **Egypt** and **Syria** joined in the **United Arab Republic** in 1958, but **Syria** seceded in 1961. **Israel**'s defeat of **Egypt** in the **Six-Day War** of 1967 dealt Nasser a severe blow, but the Egyptian public would not accept his offer to resign. He died in 1970 shortly after mediating a crisis between **King Hussein** of **Jordan** and the **PLO.**

NATIONAL PACT, in 1946, was an unwritten power-sharing agreement in which leaders of **Lebanon**'s Maronite Christians and Sunni Muslims decided that the president of **Lebanon** would always be a Maronite, the prime minister a Sunni, and the speaker of the national assembly a Shi'ite. The basis of the agreement was the census of 1936, which ranked the communities in this way by population. No census has been taken since that time, but by the mid-1970s, when the civil war broke out, specialists agreed that the demographic balance had shifted in favor of the Muslims and that the Shi'ites had become the largest community. Nevertheless, the provisional settlement of the civil war in 1990 still left **Lebanon** with a Christian president and Sunni prime minister.

NORTH AFRICA is the area stretching from the Atlantic Ocean to the Red Sea and from the Mediterranean Sea to the southern fringes of the Sahara desert. North African countries include **Egypt, Libya, Tunisia, Algeria,** and **Morocco.** The Arabic term *Maghrib,* or "West," is often used for the North African countries west of **Libya.**

OAPEC (ORGANIZATION OF ARAB PETROLEUM EXPORTING COUNTRIES) was established in 1968 by **Saudi Arabia, Kuwait,** and **Libya** to co-

During the 1970s, the Organization of Petroleum Exporting Countries (OPEC) drove up the price of oil to unprecedented levels, causing worldwide inflation. Prices came back down in the 1980s.

ordinate economic and political oil policies; other countries joined later. In October 1973, OAPEC inaugurated the era of rapid price increases by cutting back production as a lever to force **Israel** to withdraw from the territories occupied in 1967. Subsequent price increases were engineered by **OPEC.**

OCTOBER WAR was an Arab-Israeli conflict that began with an Egyptian surprise attack across the **Suez Canal** on October 6, 1973, on the Jewish Day of Atonement (Yom Kippur) and during the Muslim month of holy fasting, Ramadan. The Bar Lev Line, an elaborate network of fortifications built by **Israel** to protect the Sinai peninsula which it had captured in the **Six-Day War** of 1967, was quickly overwhelmed; and Egyptian forces advanced several miles into Sinai. Simultaneously, Syrian forces attacked the Israeli-occupied **Golan Heights.** Fighting ended on October 22 (Syrian front) and October 24 (Egyptian front) with the Arab armies substantially defeated, and a major Egyptian army surrounded by Israeli forces that had recrossed the **Suez Canal.** U.S.-mediated disengagement agreements followed. The war demonstrated Arab willingness to confront **Israel,** and the initial Arab successes showed that the Israelis were not unbeatable.

OPEC (ORGANIZATION OF PETROLEUM EXPORTING COUNTRIES) was founded in 1960 and came to include most major petroleum-exporting countries by the 1970s. Until 1974, OPEC was mostly concerned with trying to gain greater shares in oil profits for the exporting countries and in persuading foreign companies to relinquish control to host countries in a staged, orderly fashion in order to avoid outright nationalization. As the countries' control over oil production grew, they became capable of controlling prices. Rapid price rises during and after 1974 set off the transfer of enormous amounts of money from the consuming nations to the producing nations. Higher prices also provoked more exploration worldwide, which resulted in a glut that brought prices back down in the early 1980s. Since then, OPEC, under the influence of its largest producer, **Saudi Arabia,** has opted for production quotas and stable, moderate prices.

OPERATION PEACE IN GALILEE was the name given by the **Israel** Defense Force (IDF) to its invasion of **Lebanon** in 1982. Galilee, the northern district of **Israel,** was threatened by Palestinian guerrilla raids across the Lebanese frontier. The IDF's plan was to defeat the **PLO** and drive it out of **Lebanon. Israel** would then rely on a conservative Maronite government in **Lebanon** to police the border and prevent further raids. The **PLO** was successfully, though only temporarily, driven from **Lebanon.** The installation of an Israeli-paid and -supplied South Lebanon Army, composed mostly of Christians, in what **Israel** called a "security zone" extending nine miles inside southern **Lebanon** gave assurance against further attacks on Israeli towns in Galilee. Other aspects of the war went less well when world opinion disapproved of **Israel**'s siege of Beirut and connivance in the mass killing of Palestinian civilians in the Sabra and Shatila refugee camps.

PAHLAVI, SHAH MOHAMMED REZA (1919–1980) was 22 when his father, Reza Shah Pahlavi, a military commander who founded **Iran**'s Pahlavi dynasty in 1925, was deposed by Britain in 1941. European-educated Mohammed Reza Shah had a reputation as a playboy and ruled rather ineffectively until 1953, when **U.S.** and British intelligence forces helped save his throne from a nationalist movement focussed on Prime Minister **Mohammed Mossadegh.** Thereafter Mohammed Reza Shah skillfully crafted an image as a dominant absolute monarch and tried to better his standing through reforms known as the Shah-People Revolution. Close relations with the U.S., which saw him as a bulwark against Communism, did not prevent him from joining in **OPEC**'s oil price increases after 1974. The resulting flood of oil wealth into **Iran** set off a massive modernization and militarization program. Domestic opposition to the Shah and his dictatorial methods increased during this period, leading to the Iranian Revolution and his expulsion from the country in 1979. He died in exile in **Egypt.**

The coronation of the Shah of Iran and his wife took place in 1967, 26 years after the Shah came to power.

PALESTINE. Though its name derives from Roman times, and before that from the Philistines mentioned in the Bible, modern Palestine emerged from the defeat of the Ottoman Empire in World War I. After the war, Britain secured from the League of Nations a mandate over the territory south of **Lebanon** and north of **Egypt**'s Sinai peninsula between the Mediterranean Sea and the Transjordanian desert. Britain carved the emirate Transjordan (now the Hashemite Kingdom of **Jordan**) out of the eastern part of the Palestine mandate. In the remaining area between the sea and the Jordan River, they sought to fulfill a wartime commitment to foster a Jewish "national home" while not alienating the Arab population. Arabs and Zionists both felt cheated and manipulated by the British. Sporadic acts of violence between the two communities grew into an Arab rebellion in the late 1930s; simultaneously, Zionist underground groups assaulted British occupation forces. Weakened by World War II, Britain announced in 1947 that it would withdraw from Palestine and turn it over to the **United Nations.** The **United Nations General Assembly** then voted to partition the land between a Jewish state and an Arab state. **Israel** declared its independence and faced immediate war with the surrounding Arab states. The Palestinian Arab state never came into existence.

PALESTINE LIBERATION ORGANIZATION (PLO) was established in the spring of 1964 under the auspices of the **Arab League** as the political organ of the Palestinian Arabs. Its covenant, or national charter, affirms the Palestinians' right to their homeland of **Palestine,** rejects the existence of **Israel,** and vows to combat Zionism. This document was effectively superseded by subsequent PLO decisions to accept **Resolutions 242** and **338** recognizing **Israel**'s existence and by calls for establishment of a Palestinian state only in the **Gaza Strip** and **West Bank,** but it has never been formally amended or disavowed. Though the PLO was intended to control a Palestine Liberation Army, the units actually formed were controlled by other Arab states. In 1969, **Yasir Arafat,** the leader of the guerrilla group **al-Fatah,** became chairman of the PLO's executive body. He has skillfully held together many factions advocating different political viewpoints. Driven from **Jordan** in 1970 and from **Lebanon** in 1982, the PLO finally moved its headquarters to Tunis where it is far removed from immediate confrontation with **Israel.**

PALESTINIAN REFUGEES. Of the approximately 1.3 million Arabs living in mandate **Palestine** at the outbreak of the first Arab-Israeli war in 1948, 600,000 to 650,000 became refugees, two-thirds moving to the **West Bank** and **Gaza Strip,** 100,000 to **Jordan,** and 150,000 to **Syria** and **Lebanon.** When **Israel** captured the **West Bank** in 1967, well over 200,000 more Palestinians fled to **Jordan.** Most of these refugees and their descendants have never gained citizenship status in another country, and many still live in refugee camps established by the **United Nations. Israel** has long maintained that the refugees of 1948 fled because Arab leaders ordered or urged them to do so. Palestinians charge that, for the most part, they were driven from their homes by **Israel.** Israeli diaries and memoirs published in recent years at least in part support the Palestinian claim.

PEOPLE'S DEMOCRATIC REPUBLIC OF YEMEN (PDRY), also known as South Yemen, united in 1990 with the Yemen Arab Republic to form the single country of **Yemen.** A bit larger than New Mexico and almost twice the size of the Yemen Arab Republic, South Yemen occupied the southern coast of the **Arabian peninsula** from the port of Aden, its capital at the mouth of the Red Sea, to the border of Oman. Its population at the time of union was about 2.5 million. Although Aden had been a British crown colony, Britain had exercised looser control over the tribal lands to the east, which included the fertile Hadramaut valley. The British tried to create a tribally dominated federation in the area after 1959, but a leftist resistance movement based on the Aden labor union initiated an armed rebellion that forced the British to withdraw entirely and grant independence in 1967. A Communist government linked to the Soviet Union soon came to power. It supported an unsuccessful revolt against the Sultan of Oman in the Omani province of Dhufar and had tempestuous relations, including border wars and attempts at union, with the Yemen Arab Republic.

PERSIAN GULF is a 90,000-square-mile body of water running northwestward from the Gulf of Oman and the Arabian Sea; it separates **Iran** from various Arab states. Its length from the **Shatt al-Arab** in the northwest to the **Strait of Hormuz** in the southeast is about 600 miles. Despite its desert shores, the Persian Gulf has been a center of international trade and pearl fishing since ancient times; it is the only point of maritime access to Mesopotamia, modern **Iraq.** In recent decades, great amounts of oil have been found around and beneath it. This has made it a major center for shipping and an area of serious military concern both for its bordering countries, and for countries like the **United States** that consume the oil exported through it. Some Arabs insist that it should be called the Arabian Gulf, but long historical practice favors the term Persian Gulf.

PHALANGE (*KATA'IB*) is a Christian Lebanese political organization established in 1936 by Pierre Gemayel (Jumayyil) and others. Starting as a youth group, the Phalange evolved into a political faction and then an armed militia during the 1960s and 1970s. Phalange ideology has stressed the primacy of Lebanese interests over all-Arab interests. The Phalange opposed the growth of **PLO** power in **Lebanon** after 1970. During the 1982 Israeli invasion, the Phalange cooperated openly with **Israel,** which had long been secretly supporting them. The founder's son, Bashir, was elected president of **Lebanon** in 1982, but was assassinated before taking office. His brother Amin then became president. Splits within the Phalange political and military leadership weakened the Phalange in the late 1980s, and its power was finally broken by Lebanese army commander General Michel Aoun, who was then overwhelmed by **Syria** in 1990.

PLO. See **Palestine Liberation Organization.**

QADHDHAFI, MU'AMMAR (1942–   ) was born to a poor tribal family in southern **Libya** and, in 1963, graduated from the Military Academy. In 1969, he played a leading role in the overthrow of the Libyan monarchy. He was promptly promoted to colonel and assumed a number of leadership posts which, under one title or another, have made him the ruler of **Libya** down to today. He was deeply influenced by the nationalist ideology of **Egypt**'s **Nasser** and has tried through his political writings, military means, and buying influence with **Libya**'s oil wealth to make himself a central figure in Arab and world affairs. He is regarded by fellow Arabs and non-Arabs alike as an erratic leader. Still, **Libya,** under Qadhdhafi, has prospered, despite police-state controls.

QATAR is a tiny emirate located on a Connecticut-sized desert peninsula that juts into the **Persian Gulf** from the **Arabian Peninsula.** Qatar came under British domination early in the 20th century. Oil production began in 1949, thus making Qatar an oil state well before any discoveries in the neighboring **United Arab Emirates (UAE).** Unable to reach agreement on terms for joining the **UAE** when it was formed in 1971, Qatar became an independent country with its capital at Doha. The Emir of Qatar rules over 257,081 people, two-thirds of whom are foreign workers.

RAFSANJANI, ALI AKBAR HASHEMI (1934–) is the current president of the Islamic Republic of **Iran.** Hojatalislam (his rank as a religious scholar) Hashemi Rafsanjani trained as a cleric and became active politically as a follower of **Ayatollah Khomeini** in 1963. He was imprisoned under the Shah but was an active high-level organizer during the 1979 revolution. He held many positions in the new revolutionary government, including commander-in-chief of the armed forces during the final year of the **Iran-Iraq War.** He is the leader of the pragmatic moderate faction in the Iranian government.

RAMADAN WAR. See **October War.**

REAGAN, RONALD (1911–). U.S. president (1981–89) whose administration was marked by a highly publicized concern with **terrorism** that culminated in the American retaliatory bombing of **Libya** in 1986; strong support for **Israel,** despite temporary reservations caused by popular disapproval of the 1982 Israeli invasion of **Lebanon;** and the landing of American troops in **Lebanon** in 1982 to oversee **Israel**'s disengagement. The latter enterprise ended quickly once the **U.S.** became involved in Lebanese factional fighting and suffered heavy losses in bombing attacks on its embassy and a marine barracks in Beirut. Secretly, the Reagan administration also undertook to sell weapons to **Iran,** a country publicly ful-

U.S. president Ronald Reagan (shown below with King Fahd of Saudi Arabia) came to office on the same day (January 20, 1981) that the hostages in Iran were released.

minated against, in order to facilitate the release of hostages in **Lebanon;** the proceeds from the arms sales were used to fund anti-communist guerrillas in Nicaragua. Revelation of this scandal helped prompt Reagan to tilt toward **Iraq** in the **Iran-Iraq War,** despite the dictatorial character of the Iraqi regime.

SABAH, SHEIK JABER AL- (1926–   ), emir of **Kuwait** since 1978 and a member of the Sabah family that has ruled **Kuwait** since 1859. He was little known to the general public before the **Persian Gulf** crisis of 1990; the invasion of **Kuwait** by **Iraq** forced him into exile. Since his return, he has gained a reputation for caution, conservatism, and reticence.

SADAT, ANWAR (1918–1981), the president of **Egypt** from 1970-81. Sadat was raised in an Egyptian village and received his military training at the Egyptian military academy. Politically active, he joined the **Muslim Brotherhood** and other activist organizations and was imprisoned twice. He joined **Gamal Abd al-Nasir's (Nasser's) Free Officers Movement** and participated in the revolution of 1952. After holding a number of government posts, he was appointed vice president in 1969, apparently because **Nasser** wanted to balance the leftist forces in his regime. When **Nasser** died in September 1970, Sadat succeeded him as president, but he was not firmly in power until he suppressed a leftist coup eight months later. Sadat terminated **Egypt's** close military relationship with the **U.S.S.R.** and restored **Egypt's** pride by attacking **Israel,** with initial success, in the **October War** of 1973. Efforts to liberalize the economy and move away from socialism were less successful. His November 1977 visit to **Jerusalem,** followed by the signing of the **Camp David Accords** and the Egyptian-Israeli peace treaty, dramatically altered the balance of power in the Middle East and earned Sadat the hatred of many Arabs even as the rest of the world hailed him as a peacemaker. Muslim radicals assassinated him at a military parade in October 1981.

Egyptian president Anwar Sadat (below at left meeting with U.S. secretary of state Henry Kissinger in 1974) earned the hatred of many Arabs by making peace with Israel.

SADDAM'S QADISIYA is the term given by **Iraq** to the **Iran-Iraq War.** Qadisiya is the name of a battle fought early in the 7th century A.D. between an army of Muslim Arabs and the imperial army of the Iranian Shah. The Muslims won the battle and subsequently conquered the whole Persian Empire. In using the term symbolically for the **Iran-Iraq War,** the Iraqi government was trying both to compare **Saddam Hussein** with the heroes of the original Islamic conquest, and to suggest that **Iraq** was fighting nationalistically for all of the Arabs against the power of **Iran.**

SADR, MUSA AL- (1928–78) was a spiritual and political leader of **Lebanon**'s Shi'ite community. Born in **Iran** and educated in Najaf, **Iraq,** a major center of Shi'ite learning, he arrived in **Lebanon** in 1959 and took an immediate interest in charitable and social affairs. He played a leading role in the establishment of **Lebanon**'s Supreme Islamic Shi'a Council (1967) and went on to found a Shi'ite political movement (1973) and the Amal militia (1975); the latter played a major role in the Lebanese civil war. Musa al-Sadr mysteriously disappeared on August 31, 1978, on a trip to **Libya.**

SAUD, KING (1902–69) acceded to the throne of **Saudi Arabia** upon the 1953 death of his father, King Abd al-Aziz, the kingdom's founder. His extravagance and **Nasser**'s charge that he was plotting his assassination caused the Saud family to limit his powers in 1958. He tried to regain power from his half-brother Crown Prince **Faisal,** but on November 2, 1964, **Saudi Arabia**'s high religious council formally deposed him and crowned **Faisal** king. He spent the rest of his life in exile in Europe and **Egypt.**

SAUDI ARABIA is a largely desert country more than twice the size of Texas that occupies most of the **Arabian Peninsula.** Its 9 million people are concentrated in three areas: the mountains and seaports along the Red Sea; the holy cities of Mecca and Medina (also in the mountains); and in the oil region along the **Persian Gulf.** The capital, Riyadh, is in the desert interior province of Najd, the homeland of the Saud family. Between the mid-18th century and the 1920s, there were three Saudi kingdoms, each based on an alliance between tribes led by the Saud family and religious leaders supporting the conservative and puritanical interpretation of **Islam** preached in the 1740s by Muhammad ibn Abd al-Wahhab. Wahhabi (more properly Muwahhidun) enthusiasm and intolerance did not prevent the first two Saudi states from falling before Egyptian invasion (1818) or family feuding (1887). Abd al-Aziz ibn Saud rebuilt the state in the 1920s and declared the Kingdom of Saudi Arabia in 1932. From the 1960s onward, oil wealth transformed the kingdom into a wealthy, modern, pro-Western, but still rigidly puritanical and intolerant state.

SHAMIR, YITZHAK (1915–   ) was born in Poland (original last name Yzernitzky) and immigrated to **Palestine** in 1935. He first joined **Menahem Begin**'s Irgun underground but left it to join Lehi, a violent underground group also known as the Stern Gang after its founder Alexander Stern. After **Israel** became independent, Shamir became a leading figure in the Mossad intelligence organization. He joined **Begin**'s Herut Party in 1970 and succeeded to the office of prime minister when **Begin** retired in 1983. He has since been the dominant figure in Israeli politics and an adamant defender of right-wing policies, most notably the retention of the territories occupied in 1967.

SHATT AL-ARAB is a river about 120 miles long formed by the juncture of the Tigris and Euphrates Rivers in southern **Iraq;** it flows to the **Persian Gulf** and forms part of the boundary between **Iran** and **Iraq.** As **Iraq**'s most important maritime outlet and a vital waterway for the Iranian oil industry centered on Abadan, control of the Shatt al-Arab has long been a bone of contention between the two countries. In the Algiers agreement of 1975, **Iraq** agreed to recognize the middle of the river as the boundary in return for **Iran**'s termination of assistance to rebellious Iraqi **Kurds.** At the onset of the **Iran-Iraq War** in 1980, **Iraq** annulled the agreement, claiming that **Iran** had violated some of its particulars. As opposition to the Iraqi occupation of **Kuwait** increased in 1990, **Iraq** once again accepted the principle of joint use of the waterway. War wreckage, however, has left it largely unpassable.

SIX-DAY WAR had its roots in border tensions between **Israel** and its Arab neighbors, tensions that intensified in the mid-1960s and came to a head in mid-May 1967. At that time, **Egypt**'s **Gamal Abd al-Nasir (Nasser)** ordered the **United Nations** Emergency Force (UNEF) that had been watching the Egyptian-Israeli border since 1956 to withdraw. Although much of **Egypt**'s army was in **Yemen** supporting the republican side of the civil war there, **Nasser** kept taunting and challenging **Israel.** Whether he wanted or expected war is unknown, but on June 5, 1967, **Israel** launched devastating preemptive attacks on Egyptian and Syrian airfields. Having secured air superiority, **Israel** easily defeated the Egyptians, Syrians, and Jordanians on the ground. When a ceasefire was accepted by all parties on June 10, **Israel** was left in possession of the **Golan Heights** on the Syrian front, the **West Bank** on the Jordanian front, and the **Gaza Strip** and Sinai peninsula on the Egyptian front.

STRAIT OF HORMUZ at the entrance of the **Persian Gulf** is a major chokepoint for oil shipments. There was great fear that **Iran** would somehow close the strait during the **Iran-Iraq War** despite the virtual impossibility of accomplishing this without a strong navy. The shipping channel of the 30-mile-wide strait runs through Omani territorial waters and is quite distant from the nearest Iranian island.

SUEZ CANAL, the 101-mile-long canal connecting the Red Sea with the Mediterranean Sea which, when opened in 1869, enabled ships for the first time to sail directly to India and China without going around Africa. **Egypt** quickly became a focus of European political attention, and when **Egypt** fell into debt, Britain bought its share of the canal company. Thus the canal, designed by Ferdinand de Lesseps and built with Egyptian labor, was owned primarily by French and British investors and the British government. **Gamal Abd al-Nasir (Nasser)** nationalized the canal in July 1956, in retaliation for the withholding of economic aid by Western countries. At the end of October of that year, following a secret agreement with Britain and France, **Israel** invaded the Sinai peninsula. A few days later British and French forces landed in the Canal Zone, ostensibly to protect the canal but actually to cut off Egyptian reinforcements and guarantee an Israeli victory. **U.S.** and **U.S.S.R.** pressure forced the invaders to withdraw and the canal reopened, only to close once more when **Israel** again captured the Sinai peninsula in 1967. The canal did not again reopen until after the **October War** of 1973.

SYRIA stretches from the Mediterranean Sea to beyond the Euphrates River, forming the link between what was known as Mesopotamia and the lands of the eastern Mediterranean. An Oklahoma-sized country with a population of 11 million (85 percent Muslim, the rest Christian), Syria is one of the most historic parts of the Middle East. Damascus, its capital, and Aleppo are among the oldest cities in the world. After World War I, France overcame the resistance of a newly proclaimed Arab kingdom and conquered Syria, which it then ruled under a League of Nations mandate until 1946. Plagued by coups and political unrest, Syria joined with **Egypt** in the **United Arab Republic** between 1958 and 1961. The **Ba'th Party** took over in 1963, and the current ruler, **Hafiz al-Asad,** consolidated his power in 1970. Syria has been an intransigent foe of **Israel** and has relied heavily upon military and political support from the **U.S.S.R.** Syria first intervened in **Lebanon**'s civil war in 1976; by 1990, when Syria suppressed the last major Lebanese military force, it dominated **Lebanon** completely. Syria's relations with **Iraq,** which is ruled by another branch of the **Ba'th Party,** have been very bitter, a situation which has helped foster good relations with **Iraq**'s enemy, **Iran.**

TERRORISM. Many Middle East nations use fear of military or police action to suppress internal opposition (**Iraq, Syria, Iran, Israel** in the occupied territories) or intimidate external enemies (**Israel, Libya**). Some people call this "state terrorism," though it is not an unusual practice worldwide. Terrorism proper is a belief in the use of fear to achieve political ends when the fear is, in fact, beyond the terrorists' ability to carry out. A state that bombs a town once may realistically be expected to bomb it again. By contrast, terrorists usually have little capacity to commit much more violence than their immediate act. They depend upon wide publicity to magnify their potential power and frighten people enough to grant their political demands. Typically the weapon of small, weak groups, such as the Palestinian and other guerrilla organizations, terrorism became an important part of Middle Eastern politics from the 1960s onward, largely because of the enormous publicity given it by Western govenments and news media, and the willingness of the general public to believe exaggerated estimates of terrorist strength. Most organizations eventually abandon terrorism as unproductive.

In the 1980s, terrorism directed against U.S. civilians often took the form of airplane hijackings (above).

TRUMAN, HARRY (1884–1972) was the **U.S** president whose term (1945–1953) marked the beginning of substantial **U.S.** involvement in the Middle East. In the name of thwarting Soviet expansion, Truman gave economic aid (the Truman Plan) to Greece and **Turkey,** and he supported **Iran's** demand that the **U.S.S.R.** withdraw its occupying forces from that country. As a supporter of Zionism, he also worked to persuade **U.N.** members to vote for the partition of **Palestine**—the necessary first step toward an independent **Israel.**

TUNISIA is a Florida-sized country tucked between **Libya** and **Algeria** at the waist of the Mediterranean. Its 7 million people are almost entirely Arab Muslim. From Roman times through the early modern era, Tunisia was traditionally the political center of **North Africa** east of **Morocco.** The ruins of ancient Carthage are located just outside the present capital of Tunis. France invaded and established a protectorate over Tunisia in 1881; not until 1955 did the country escape French control. A republic came into being in 1957. Independent Tunisia was dominated by **Habib Bourguiba** and the Neo-Destour Party until party leaders removed him from office in 1987.

TURKEY, one of the largest countries of the Middle East, arose from the defeated Ottoman Empire at the end of World War I. At the time, the victorious allies tried to limit the Turks to a small, landlocked state inside Anatolia (Asia Minor). Led by Mustafa Kemal, however, the Turks fought to extend their territory over all of Anatolia and a small part of Europe outside the city of Istanbul, the old Ottoman capital. Mustafa Kemal established the Turkish Republic in 1923 as a country somewhat larger than Texas with its capital at Ankara in central Anatolia. Turkey has a population of 52 million (mostly Turks but also many **Kurds** and some Armenians and other minorities). Kemal followed the late Ottoman policy of imitating Europe by adopting nationalism and secularism as the state ideology and suppressing Islamic institutions. Turkey has sought closer ties with Europe and, after becoming a NATO member following World War II, has become less and less involved with the affairs of other Middle Eastern countries.

UNION OF SOVIET SOCIALIST REPUBLICS (U.S.S.R.). The long-term czarist Russian and then Soviet aim of expanding southward, hopefully far enough to secure access to warm water ports, prompted the Soviet Union to take an interest in **Iran** and **Turkey** after World War II. Iranian distrust of the U.S.S.R. was aroused in 1946 when the Soviets delayed their promised military withdrawal from **Iran.** Both the Shah's **Iran** and the Islamic Republic of **Iran** remained suspicious of Soviet intentions. Similary, **Turkey** joined NATO to resist Soviet influence. The Arab countries, however, saw the U.S.S.R. as a means of balancing American influence. In the late 1950s, **Egypt, Syria,** and **Iraq** accepted Soviet friendship and military support, as later did **Libya,** the **People's Democratic Republic of Yemen,** and the **PLO.** Yet most Arab countries continued to fear and suppress domestic Communist parties. Soviet arms enabled the Arabs to challenge **Israel** in 1967 and 1973, and **Iraq** to challenge **Iran** in 1980. As the U.S.S.R. underwent internal dissolution and the cold war evaporated from 1989 onward, the Arabs' expectations of Soviet military and political

Once the Soviet Union relaxed its emigration policies, thousands of Soviet Jews began moving to Israel, taxing Israel's already difficult economic situation.

support fell, leading to a greater willingness to accept American leadership, as represented by the Madrid peace conference of 1991. In late 1991, the **U.S.S.R.** ceased to exist, and instead became a commonwealth of independent states.

UNITED ARAB EMIRATES (UAE). During the 19th century, in order to protect its trade with India, Great Britain forced treaties upon a number of Arab tribes living along the coast of the lower **Persian Gulf.** Britain controlled the political and military affairs of these states, but they otherwise continued as small, poor, desert principalities. With the dissolution of the British Empire after World War II, the British encouraged the hereditary emirs of the principalities to join in a single federation. The United Arab Emirates, occupying an area about the size of South Carolina, was declared independent in 1971. Meanwhile, however, oil had been discovered in 1958. Three of the seven emirates—Abu Dhabi (also the name of the UAE's capital city), Dubai, and Sharja—export oil, Abu Dhabi being the richest, largest, and most heavily populated. The other four emirates, Ajman, Umm Qaiwain, Ra's al-Khaima, and Fujaira occupy territory on and near the mountainous Musandam peninsula at the **Strait of Hormuz.** The population of the UAE is 1.6 million, only 20 percent of whom are Arabs native to the region. Foreign workers, half of them from India and Pakistan and mostly male, make up the bulk of the population. Oil wealth has made the UAE (particularly Abu Dhabi) one of the richest countries per capita in the world.

UNITED ARAB REPUBLIC (UAR) was the union of **Egypt** and **Syria** that took place in February 1958. The union lasted until September 1961, when **Syria** seceded after a military coup. Arab nationalist ideology had long favored the union of Arab states; and given **Gamal Abd al-Nasir's (Nasser's)** great popularity as ruler of **Egypt,** this seemed like a first step in achieving that dream. But in actuality, the Syrians felt exploited and neglected by the arrangement.

UNITED NATIONS GENERAL ASSEMBLY is the main body of the United Nations in which every member nation has a vote. The General Assembly has acted many times on Middle Eastern matters, including voting to partition **Palestine** in 1947; but its votes rarely have the impact of votes in the **United Nations Security Council.** The General Assembly has frequently expressed support for Palestinian positions in the Arab-Israeli dispute and has granted the **PLO** permanent observer status.

UNITED NATIONS RESOLUTIONS 242 AND 338. In November 1967, following the **Six-Day War,** the **United Nations Security Council** voted for Resolution 242. This resolution called for "a just and lasting peace in which every state in the area can live in security" and declared "the inadmissability of the acquisition of territory by war." It specifically called for Israeli withdrawal "from territories" occupied during the war. The latter phrase permitted subsequent disagreement on whether *all* territories or only *some* territories were meant. In 1973, the **Security Council** passed Resolution 338, which reiterated 242 but added that peace negotiations should be carried out under "appropriate auspices." The Madrid peace conference of 1991 was convened on the basis of Resolutions 242 and 338.

UNITED NATIONS SECURITY COUNCIL is the U.N. body charged with taking action in matters affecting international peace, such as wars. The **U.S., U.S.S.R.,** Great Britain, France, and the People's Republic of China are permanent members. The remaining 10 members are elected on a rotating basis. The Security Council has acted in many Middle Eastern conflicts, including calling for ceasefires in several Arab-Israeli wars and in the **Iran-Iraq War,** establishing peace-keeping and truce observer forces in **Lebanon** and elsewhere, and authorizing formation of the coalition that defeated **Iraq** in the Persian Gulf War. During the cold war, the **U.S.,** Britain, and France often disagreed with the **U.S.S.R.** and China

In January 1991, U.N. Secretary General Perez de Cuellar (below left) met with Middle East leaders in a last-ditch attempt to avoid the outbreak of the Persian Gulf War.

in the Security Council. This paralyzed the Council because each of the five permanent members has the power to veto resolutions.

UNITED STATES had few interests in the Middle East prior to World War II. Postwar interests quickly centered on oil production, with many U.S. American companies active in exploration in the region; the state of **Israel,** which President **Truman** strongly supported; and opposition to Soviet and Communist influence. With the growth of nationalism in the area, many Middle Easterners came to look on the United States with suspicion or hostility, precisely because of the presence of U.S. oil companies and American support for **Israel.** Anti-communist, pro-American regimes appeared to be tools of imperialist manipulation, and the U.S. was increasingly seen as playing the imperialist role that Britain had played before the war. The U.S. was best liked in **Iran** and the **Arabian Peninsula;** Soviet-supported **Egypt** (until **Anwar Sadat**), **Syria,** and **Iraq** were most unfriendly. The Persian Gulf War of 1991, though thought by some to be part of an American plot, increased U.S. prestige and political influence in all parts of the region to a level theretofore unknown.

VALI FAQIH, the key governing institution of the Islamic Republic of **Iran,** was first elaborated in lectures given by **Ayatollah Khomeini** in 1969 during his exile in **Iraq** and subsequently published in his book on Islamic government. **Khomeini** maintained that a superior religious authority was necessary in a state to control the natural drift of secular governments toward corruption and dictatorship. He called this authority *vilayet-i faqih,* or "the governance of a religious jurist," and the individual exercising it the *vali faqih, vali* meaning "governor" and *faqih* meaning "scholar of Islamic religious law." Although many Shi'ite scholars disagreed with **Khomeini**'s theory, it was incorporated into the constitution of the Islamic Republic, and **Khomeini** himself served in this position until his death. He was then succeeded by his student **Ayatollah Ali Hosseini-Khamenei.** The powers of the *vali faqih* include declaring war, concluding peace, appointing key judges, and removing a president from office after impeachment by the Majles (National Assembly). The *vali faqih* does not have day-to-day governing powers, however, and is far from being a religious dictator.

WEST BANK is a Delaware-sized area on the west bank of the Jordan River designated in the **United Nations General Assembly** resolution of 1947 as part of a projected Palestinian Arab state. The territory was captured by Jordanian forces in 1948 and annexed to **Jordan.** In 1967, **Israel** captured the territory and renamed it Judaea and Samaria, using names drawn from the Bible. Palestinian leaders have demanded that it be returned to Arab control and made into a Palestinian state. **Jordan** insisted that it be returned to Jordanian control until 1988, when **King Hussein** renounced **Jordan**'s claim in favor of the Palestinians. **Israel** claims no one owns the territory and that it is simply administering it until final ownership is determined, although the current **Likud** government of **Yitzhak Shamir** has repeatedly stated that it will not return the occupied territories. For almost 25 years, the West Bank's approximately 600,000 Arab inhabitants have been subjected to a sometimes harsh military rule and deprived of civil rights. This, highlighted by the *intifada* uprising that began in 1987,

Jewish settlers began arriving in Palestine in the late 19th century, more than 50 years before the state of Israel was established in 1948.

has set the West Bank at the center of the Arab-Israeli conflict. **Israel**'s policy of building Jewish settlements on the West Bank, its diversion of most West Bank water into **Israel**'s national water network, and the fact that without the territorial buffer of the West Bank, **Israel**'s width is only nine miles compound the difficulty of reaching a solution.

YEMEN has been, since May 1990, a single country occupying the entire southwest corner of the **Arabian Peninsula;** it has a population of around 12 million people. Before that date, the northern part of the country, with only a third of the territory but over three-quarters of the population, had been known as the Yemen Arab Republic (YAR) or North Yemen. Its capital, San'a, became the capital of the combined country. A mountainous region with a torrid coastal plain backed by lush highlands, North Yemen is historically famous as the original home of coffee—Mocha is the name of the port coffee was shipped from—but today the main crop is the qat tree, which produces a mildly narcotic, chewable leaf. North Yemen was an independent country ruled by a Shi'ite religious leader called an Imam until 1962, when a revolution established the YAR and set off eight years of civil war. When **Saudi Arabia** became rich, millions of Yemenis went there to work. The wages they sent home were crucial to the Yemeni economy, though otherwise YAR relations with **Saudi Arabia** and PDRY (South Yemen) were uneven. **Saudi Arabia** expelled the Yemeni workers during the Persian Gulf War because Yemen sympathized with **Iraq,** but by then Yemen had begun to export newly found oil and was embarking, united at last, on a new phase of its history.

YISHUV refers to the Jewish population of **Palestine** before the establishment of the state of **Israel** in 1948. The Yishuv was formed by several waves (*aliyot* in Hebrew) of immigration. The first *aliyah* in the late 19th century brought about 25,000 Jews to **Palestine.** The second *aliyah*, between 1904 and 1914, added another 50,000. By 1948, approximately 580,000 Jews had immigrated.

YOM KIPPUR WAR. See October War.

A Moment in History

The Middle East is a region of crisis. But behind the headlines of terrorism and slaughter, living amid the wars and revolutions that plague the region, are millions of people—everyday people who must eke out an existence in an atmosphere of impending catastrophe. Most of the people living in the Middle East have no more power to stop the violence or alleviate their oppression than we do to house our homeless or eliminate the crime in our streets. Through no fault of their own, the people of the Middle East are caught up in the political rivalries and religious and ethnic tensions discussed earlier in this book.

There are more people in the Middle East than in the United States, and the land they inhabit is more extensive. A select few see their lives improving. For the most part, these people either live in countries blessed by oil wealth and small populations or, through education and family connections, have been able to move into elite positions in their societies. A handful have benefited by working in the oppressive agencies of dictatorial governments.

A far larger proportion of the population, however, remains poor and is ever fearful of growing poorer. In the larger countries such as Egypt, Iran, and Algeria, economic growth has a difficult time keeping up with the burgeoning population. For people in this situation, the political arena is a spectacle of hope and fear. The poor look to their leaders to find the path to the glorious future that's been promised to them. At the same time, they harbor great anxiety over imperialist conspiracies—often focusing on the United States—that they see besetting their countries.

Heightened American prestige in the Middle East following the Persian Gulf War has provided the U.S. with a limited window of opportunity during which to pursue foreign-policy goals.

Crisis they know can lead to chaos. For every person who believes that chaos may ultimately bring positive change, there are a dozen more whose worries about their jobs and families override such hopes.

The United States has long been concerned with its own "vital interests" in the Middle East: the continuity of oil supplies, the blocking of Soviet influence, and the security of Israel. Now, with U.S. prestige heightened in the aftermath of the war against Iraq, American policymakers perceive a window of opportunity—however limited—in which to pursue and/or implement a number of foreign-policy goals. Foremost among these is the possibility of solving the Israeli-Arab dilemma through negotiation, a process perhaps now in its infancy with the Madrid Peace Conference in late 1991. At the same time, the U.S. also hopes to encourage the growth of democratic institutions, curtail the proliferation of dangerous weapons, humble Saddam Hussein as a warning to other ambitious dictators, and arrange permanently for the world supply of inexpensive oil. The U.S. has already achieved one of its most important goals: the release of American hostages from Lebanon, some of whom had been in captivity for over seven years.

For some, this American vision has elements of nobility and altruism. But for the many peoples who live in the Middle East, that same vision can seem imperialistic and conspiratorial. Many Iranians, for instance, still see the United States as the "Great Satan," an evil force that has ignored their country's help in the Persian Gulf War. Iraqis feel only bitterness at American determination to destroy their leader or, more precisely, America's inability (in their view) to tolerate an Arab leader

The continuing talks between Arabs and Israelis may help resolve some of the region's more pressing problems, including the intifada *uprising and other issues involving the Palestinians.*

The Middle East is home to many more people than is the United States. Ultimately, the people of the Middle East must—and indeed will—determine their own destiny.

who dares aspire to greatness. In Egypt, members of the Christian minority, while happy that the United States is helping their country economically, might also feel that Americans do not understand the danger looming for Egypt's Christians if Muslim activists continue to gain political influence. The typical Jordanian scorns U.S. indifference to the fate of the Palestinians and America's blind support for Israeli government policy. Jewish settlers on the West Bank worry that someday, perhaps as soon as tomorrow, the old specter of anti-semitism will reemerge in the United States and that Israel will be abandoned politically to the Arabs in return for oil. Even in Western-leaning Turkey, the prevailing attitude in many circles is that the United States, like all the Western countries, hates Islam and will do anything to prevent true Muslims from asserting their social and political values.

Nationalists and Muslim activists alike believe that they have been manipulated and abused by the West for the past two centuries, and there is much to substantiate their view. The United States must always bear in mind that it is not loved in the Middle East. In confronting the bewildering complex of crises in the Middle East, the United States must try to act wisely and to be aware of the problems and sensitivities of the people.

Ultimately the myriad peoples of the Middle East must and will make their own future. Victory in the Persian Gulf War has produced a moment in history when it might be possible to loosen some of the region's snarled knots. Soon this moment will pass, and the people of the Middle East will be left to resume their own rendezvous with history.

INDEX

ILLUSTRATION CREDITS

The following list acknowledges, according to page, the sources of illustrations used in the LANDS AND PEOPLES SPECIAL EDITION: CRISIS IN THE MIDDLE EAST. The credits are listed illustration by illustration — top to bottom, left to right. When the name of the photographer has been listed with the source, the two are separated by a slash. If two or more illustrations appear on the same page, their credits are separated by semicolons.

2 © Abbas/Magnum
5 © George Rodger/Magnum
7 © Courtesy, United Nations Relief and Works
    Agency for Palestine Refugees
8 © Reuters/Bettmann
9 © Courtesy, United Nations
10 © Wide World Photos
11 © Adventurier/Gamma-Liaison
12 © Wide World Photos
15 © UPI/Bettmann
16 © Roland Neveu/Gamma-Liaison
17 © Gad Gross/JB Pictures
18 © Gilles Bassignac/Gamma-Liaison
19 © Wide World Photos
20 © D. Aubert/Sygma
21 © Wesley Bocxe/Sipa Press
22 © UPI/Bettmann;
    © Wide World Photos
23 © FPG International
24 © Burt Glinn/Magnum;
    © UPI;
    © UPI/Bettmann
25 © UPI/Bettmann
26 © Roger Coral/Magnum;
    © Peter Skingley/UPI/Bettmann;
    © FPG International
27 © UPI/Bettmann;
    © UPI/Bettmann
28 © Gamma-Liaison;
    © UPI/Bettmann;
    © UPI/Bettmann;
    © Wide World Photos
29 © David Burnett/Gamma-Liaison;
    © Wide World Photos
30 © Wide World Photos;
    © UPI;
    © Reuters/Bettmann
31 © Karl Schumacher/The White House/UPI;
    © UPI
32 © Wide World Photos;
    © Bisson/Sygma;
    © Frederic Neema/Reuters/Bettmann
33 © El Koussy/Sygma;
    © Eli Reed/Magnum;
    © Jim Hollander/Reuters/Bettmann
34 © Wide World Photos;
    © P. Robert/Sygma;
    © Wide World Photos
35 © Wide World Photos;
    © R. Bossu/Sygma;
    © Havakuk Levison/Reuters/Bettmann

36 © Sipa;
    © Zoltan Varro/Sygma;
    © Aladin/Reuters/Bettmann
37 © Ray Stobblebine/Reuters/Bettmann;
    © Wide World Photos
38 © Wide World Photos;
    © Alain Nogues/Sygma
39 © Rob Taggart/Reuters/Bettmann
40 © Claude Salhani/Reuters/Bettmann;
    © Sygma
41 © Wide World Photos;
    © Charles Platiau/Reuters/Bettmann
42 © P. Durand/Sygma;
    © Santiago Lyon/Reuters/Bettmann
43 © Wide World Photos;
    © Wide World Photos
44 © Wide World Photos;
    © Patrick Robert/Sygma
45 © Claude Salhan/Reuters/Bettmann
46 © Bill Cranford/UPI/Bettmann;
    © Wide World Photos
47 © Sygma
48 © Reuters/Bettmann
49 © FPG;
    © Robert Capa/Magnum Photos
50 Brown Brothers
51 © Mehmet Biber/Photo Researchers
52 © Elliott Erwitt/Magnum
53 © AP/Wide World Photos
54 © AP/Wide World Photos
55 © FPG
57 © Reuters/Bettmann
59 © Reuters/Bettmann
61 © UPI/Bettmann
62 © Sygma
63 © Abbas/Magnum
64 © AP/Wide World Photos
66 © Reuters/Bettmann
69 © Reuters/Bettmann
71 © Reuters/Bettmann
73 © UPI Bettmann
74 © Marilyn Silverstone/Magnum
77 © UPI/Bettmann
79 © Sygma
81 © Associated Press — Courtesy of ABC News
83 © Reuters/Bettmann
84 © M. Attar/Sygma
86 © UPI/Bettmann
87 © Reuters/Bettmann
88 © Reuters/Bettmann
89 © Reuters/Bettmann

Cover and title page photo: © L. Van Der Stockt/Gamma-Liaison
Contents page photos: © Wide World Photos; © Rob Taggart/Reuters/Bettmann; © Sygma; © Reuters/Bettmann

ABOUT THE AUTHOR

Dr. Richard W. Bulliet is Professor of Middle Eastern History at Columbia University in New York City. A former Guggenheim Fellow, Dr. Bulliet served as Executive Secretary of the Middle East Studies Association from 1977 to 1981, and as Director of Columbia's Middle East Institute from 1984 to 1990. He is the author of many scholarly books and novels on the Middle East, and is the editor of the journal *Iranian Studies*.